The Field Bedside Book 4

The
FIELD
BEDSIDE BOOK
4

Edited by
Wilson Stephens

Illustrated by
Richard Bradley

David & Charles

Newton Abbot   London
North Pomfret (Vt)   Vancouver

ISBN 0 7153 6837 0

Library of Congress
Catalog Card Number 75–20

825708

Set in 11 on 13pt Linotype Baskerville
and printed in Great Britain by
Latimer Trend & Company Ltd Plymouth
for David & Charles (Holdings) Limited
South Devon House Newton Abbot Devon

Published in the United States of America
by David & Charles Inc
North Pomfret Vermont 05053 USA

Published in Canada
by Douglas David & Charles Limited
132 Philip Avenue North Vancouver BC

Contents

Editor's Note

THIS IS THE FOURTH IN THE SERIES OF *The Field*'s BEDSIDE Books. Each reproduces a collection of the most popular contents in *The Field* during the preceding two years. They are chosen on the basis of the reaction of readers at the time of first appearance, giving special weight to requests for re-publication, literary merit, and general interest. The selection now presented represents roughly one item from each weekly issue, in prose and verse. Some have been condensed.

Previous *Bedside Books* have been presented in calendar sequence, with a chapter for each month. This format has now been discontinued. The new volume follows a natural but varied sequence of contents, running continuously through the year. The Contents page at the start is designed to enable readers easily to find again any article which they may wish to re-read.

Not only formal articles and poems have been included. A selection of incidental letters has been added. Most of the articles come from regular contributors to the magazine, and these brief notes are added on some of them.

D. A. Orton is our resident ornithologist; Proteus remains anonymous; Alexander specialises on games; Nimrod is the pseudonym of the keeper of A London Diary, specialising in manners and modes; Leonard Crawley is the international golfer and cricketer; D. Macer Wright combines angling with horticulture; Roy Beddington is a distinguished artist; T. B. Thomas is as Welsh as his name.

We wish good reading to all who open this book, warning them that not all its pages are soporific.

Serenading the Mule

A whiff of the past recalls a long-lost military alliance where the Ten Commandments did not apply

A GHILLIE RECOGNISED MY FISHING BAG, AND WE HAD A QUICK and extra dram. It baffles most people. This is not the haversack in which I carry tactical necessities on the river, but the larger compendium which stays in the car as the quartermaster's store of my fishing life. Some such reticule was doubtless meant when that dean of fishing bores, Izaak Walton, quacked: 'Boy, bring me my dubbing bag.'

Mine contains not merely fly-tying material. There are also apt to be assortments of reels, lines, gaff-heads, spools of nylon, hooks, tools, books, bottles, ancient chunks of beeswax, shot, spoons, floats, obsolete licences, letters from friends and, as I recently discovered, the piece of cheese which I intended to distribute to the chaffinches on the Wye several years ago but never got round to handing over. Since none of these items is visible externally, why should people look strangely at my fishing bag?

Its appearance is distinctive. It is made of rawhide. It is shaped somewhat like a small coffin. It has stalwart iron fittings and straps of particular design. These, with an odour a quarter of a century old, are the give-away. Yet only occasionally does some bystander know that he is looking at a yakdan and turn his thoughts to mules. Men who do so come of a race apart, distinctive in age-group and appearance. They are lean, their thin faces seamed and wrinkled by hot sunshine, and even more by hot winds long ago. The yakdan was, still is, the universal holdall of those who travel the high and arid Asian mountains with mules as companions and friends.

And that odour? It combines the perfumes of Arabia, and

9

of Persia and old India, too. Nor are these the artful distillations of the seraglio, but the elemental smells of lonely places east of Suez, and that is a man's world.

From where I sit the air brings in through the open window the rosiness of an English summer. But as it eddies over the top of the bookcase, my yakdan's parking place, it surrenders to the indestructible orient's smell of old times and brings to me deathless memories. That leather absorbed and is for ever giving back the sunset tang of burning dung, strong curry, griddled atta, mule sweat, man sweat, baked earth, camel harness, tamarisk and dry thorns. Shelley said that the champak odours fail like sweet thoughts in a dream. Let them go. My yakdan is good enough for me with its reminder of long days with the mule trains coughing in the dust.

'Companions and friends', I wrote earlier. It is no use being a mule's companion without also being his friend. You get nowhere if you try. A mule can sum up a man as a soldier does, both pitilessly and generously. The mule is an old soldier at heart. Let him down, laugh at him or be soft with him and you've had it, as the saying is. Be fair to him (he knows his rights as well as any barrack-room lawyer) and he does not fail his duty.

His duty? Or hers? Does it matter? It is all the same to a mule. And here, perhaps, is the clue to the singular completeness of mule character. Mules are finished articles and not, as we are, merely stages in a process of genetic change which, with each of us as a tiny stepping-stone of progress, will one day produce a superior race of men. Every mule, by contrast, is the end of his particular line of development. With no contribution to make to posterity, a mule exists only for the present. All the qualities of every ancestor come to a head, and to a full stop, in each mule.

Long-eared, long-faced, long-memoried and long of teeth (which can meet in the anatomy of a passer-by at surprising distances when these characteristics coincide), quick of heel, disciplined, bolshy, laconic, tough and independent, mules fit naturally into an army. They keep their end up. They thrive in an ambience of four-letter words, and quickly learn their significance. They become grudgingly as in all things, the natural counterparts of the p.b.i.

Few modern, technological soldiers are likely to meet them. I'm glad I did. They taught me much. No man who has ever fumbled his efforts to put a pack saddle on a critical, experienced, long-service army mule which possibly has a hangover will ever again tackle an unfamiliar task without learning the proper way first. Sometimes I stand by my yakdan, close my eyes, inhale the message-laden scent of its leather and lose all thoughts of fishing. Smell, that most evocative of the senses, starts the others going—the feel of a soft nose butting me in the back, the taste of salt trickling into my mouth, the sight of loads swaying on an uphill trail, the sound of bhoosa being munched at the end of the day. If the Indian Army ever wonder why they did not get their yakdan back, they know now.

The Gate

The five-barred gate is old and green
With lichen, and it tends to lean
Quite drunkenly between its posts
And sometimes one imagines ghosts
Might hover here some haunted night;
Two fond young lovers come to plight
Their troth, for here you still may find
Their carved initials intertwined.
Now little sandalled feet that run
To climb the bars and swing for fun;
And here the ones who came to plough
Or sow or reap would rest; and now
An old man leans to contemplate
The world beyond the five-barred gate.
MARION HOLDEN

Steam on the Farm

*A country parson analyses the traction engine cult, and finds a
new form of rural worship*

IN AUGUST 1950, AT NETTLEBED NEAR OXFORD, FARMER ARTHUR
Napper challenged his neighbour Miles Chetwynd-Stapleton
to a traction engine race. The farmer won with his 1920
Fowler engine; some 400 people watched the event. Next year
they came in their thousands to Appleford for a repeat performance and this time the late Lord Nuffield acted as starter.
A new sport was launched.

After the great drive for scrap iron during the Second
World War, it had seemed that the days of the traction
engine were numbered. Many were scrapped since their
economic use on farm and fairground had virtually ceased.
A few road rollers were still steam driven and occasionally
ploughing and threshing was steam driven but the internal-
combustion engine in tractor form had begun to take over.

In 1955 the National Traction Engine Club was formed
which I served for many years as Chairman, becoming sub-
sequently its first President. We have over 2,000 members
but there are over 40 subsidiary clubs in the British Isles and
a large number overseas. Rallies have been held in many
places (they call them re-unions overseas) and large sums have
been raised for charities, for churches, and for the fight
against disease. It has also meant the saving of hundreds of
engines from the scrapheap. Many owners in the country
have made splendid restorations, even to the point of making
spare parts themselves, although these giants were threshing,
ploughing, rolling and hauling when Victoria was on the
throne. It costs money to run an engine. Even the price of
coal is off-putting. Moreover, it costs infinite patience to bring
and keep them in safe condition.

Since my own book *Traction Engines* appeared (it was a pioneer comprehensive study) much literature has been published. There has also been a great interest in model-making, varying from the Bassett-Lowke range fired by methylated spirit to free-lance models which burn coal and are made to scale. Enthusiasts have added others of faultless design and accuracy.

At Stambourne, Essex, ploughing and cultivating by steam is not a stunt but a commercial proposition carried on in unbroken sequence since 1918 by Harold Jackson and his son Edward. Other owners also use their ploughing engines commercially when occasion demands.

People have often asked me to explain this love of steam which has captured a new and permanent host of enthusiasts whose age-group seems limitless. My own interest started when I worked with them on our farm in Suffolk long before I became a parson. Many years ago a child returned weeping from Sunday School; when asked the reason for his tears, he replied, 'Jesus wants me for a sunbeam but I still want to be an engine driver.' We are all boys at heart and owning an engine, or being a member of a club gives the opportunity to fulfil such latent ambition. Steam is silent, although an immense power is released when one hears the pleasant exhaust sound of 'tufter-tufter'.

Steam is obedient although never ferocious. A steam engine is an individual in an age of plastics and the endless belt. I have seen old specifications where the prospective owner requested his individual requirements to be incorporated into the new engine. Modern machinery, however efficient, is never lovable; on the other hand traction engines look big and splendid. Most of us will re-echo the words of Paul Jennings . . .

'. . . No Diesel has drama nor fire in her belly
No Diesel is christened Britannia nor Nelly.'

Safety at Bird Tables

*How to feed without risking accidental harm, and without giving
the undeserving cases a free-for-all*

BIRDS ARE FED IN GARDENS FOR FOUR PRINCIPAL REASONS:
one, a largely unconsidered emotional response to the sight
of cold and hungry song birds poking pathetically at the
frozen ground; two, a deliberate policy to preserve an exist-
ing level of bird population because, on aesthetic grounds,
one does not wish to see it diminish; three, a recognition that
certain species kept alive in hard weather will repay the debt
with interest when the insect pests emerge; and fourthly as
a form of 'ground baiting' to bring birds within convenient
watching distance.

How effective is this feeding? There is no doubt that, if it
is carried out judiciously, populations of small birds are preserved at a higher level than would be maintained without
it. In the absence of human intervention, hard weather
induces heavier mortality among small birds than cat, hawk,
owl and the side-effects of persistent pesticides put together.
It does so by attacking on two fronts. Small birds, like all
small warm-blooded creatures, have a heat-loss problem. To
withstand the night temperatures during a hard frost they
need to go to roost with a tankful of fuel, but that is precisely what hard weather denies them the opportunity of
doing, with their usual sustenance, animal and vegetable,
locked away under the snow or in the frost-bound earth.

From the fact that the hardest weather does not annihilate
all small birds in the affected area, even when the frost is
prolonged, one deduces that the cleverest still succeed in finding food. It follows that one does to some degree tamper with
natural selection in preserving the less survival-worthy, a
consideration unlikely to bother many. Provided feeding is

14

confined to winter, that quantities of largesse are balanced
to the climatic situation, there is no serious likelihood of
pauperising the local birds into total ineptitude. One must
provide what is convenient, then draw a firm line. Continuity
and regularity are far more important than quantity as such.

The birds people principally wish to feed are blackbirds,
song thrushes, tits of all species, finches, robins and dunnocks.
If one lives sufficiently near well-timbered open country,

woodpeckers and nuthatches may be added to the list. Wrens
and tree creepers, too, perhaps, if one could offer anything
they fancied. This I have yet to succeed in doing on any
significant scale.

Stale bread (but not mouldy) or other farinaceous matter,
well crumbled and spread, is the first resort. By crumbling
and spreading, the time otherwise taken by those feathered

garbage-cans the starlings and sparrows to clear it to the last crumb is extended sufficiently for the shyer song birds to overcome the traumas caused by the human being invading the environment to distribute the food. Provided sufficient has been supplied, they usually join the party just in the nick of time. That, of course, is a generalisation. Individual thrushes and robins may be tame enough to get in first.

All the thrushes, winter migrant species included, will benefit from windfall apples left for them in the grass. Rottenness seems to be no disadvantage. Before the price went up, dried fruit, preferably soaked before presentation, was another acceptable item for many of the thrush tribe, although not all individuals recognise its edibility. Well scattered grated cheese does robins a power of good, and blackbirds and song thrushes also take it; so will tits and the odd enterprising wren and dunnock. Bread, useful though it is as a warmth and energy source, is short fats and protein. Tits of all species, except the long tailed, and greenfinches will eat oil-rich peanuts until further orders. Either I entertain the entire East Worcestershire population, or they get through about four times their own weight daily.

The best way to frustrate sparrows is to offer the nuts in the shell, strung on stout thread. But if presented thus, there must be no gaps, or a hanged tit may be the outcome. As greenfinches may be deterred with the sparrows by this method, most people prefer to feed shelled nuts in a wire-cage feeder. The other finches present a problem. Several are highly specialised feeders. Short of planting a corner of the garden with teasels and sunflower specially for them, it is difficult to know what to do.

Buying seed, other than millet, to scatter broadcast may well lead to a weedier garden next year. If disposed to take the risk, buy only from a reputable source—a specialist. Some years ago I had the misfortune to acquire some contaminated by pesticide. There were a number of casualties, but inevitably, no sparrows or starlings. Tits and finches died, wretchedly. Last but not least, suet hung in large lumps (out of reach of foxes, etc) or in a wire-cage feeder is relished by tits, the occasional robin, woodpeckers, nuthatches, starlings.

The last thing one wishes to do by regular feeding is to establish a ready-made larder for predators. If a country dweller, one must accept the hazard of the sparrowhawk and little owl. Neither are numerically abundant; both, like the small song birds, stand in need of the food they take. The furthest one may go legally by way of deterrence is to avoid feeding their potential prey in such a way as to facilitate ambushes or unseen approaches. Place the food where there is a maximum of open ground which the predator must cross to reach its victims. Few kills are made without the advantage of surprise.

Under the Crinoline

SIR,

The first Archbishop of Wales, formerly Bishop of St Asaph for many years, told me that when he was a curate at Llangollen about a hundred years ago, he used to play croquet with my great aunts. They wore crinolines and he never forgot the way they quietly enveloped their ball and trundled it to a more favourable position.

Archbishop Edwards was a keen fisherman and, as his birthday fell just in the close season, he gave himself a special dispensation to fish on that day.

DUNCAN ROBERTSON
Llangollen, Denbighshire

Golf and the Waggle

A fine old custom, but an eminent diplomat asks, 'Should it continue to happen?'

SUCH IS THE GOLFER'S DEDICATED GULLIBILITY THAT HE MUST be a sales manager's dream. He will investigate anything that might improve his game, though he does not always do so sensibly. Sometimes he will dismantle his swing and try to put it together again more sweetly, but mostly he simply bangs balls mindlessly into the offing on the supposition that practice makes perfect.

Anyway, in the hope of a hearing and the humility of a 24-handicapper, I here present a hint which may have been overlooked in the massive scrutiny of the swing's mechanics and the body's ability to produce them with unwavering perfection. It comes from Sir John Lomax, now in his seventies:

The mechanism of focus is, in artilleryman's language, a 'dial sight' and it has a built-in range-finder. During a shot it must supply the brain with two distance and direction estimates. The one to the target is long; the other, to the ball and controlling swing, is short.

As all range-finders take time to adjust, it is wise not to overload them by multiplying the occasions which make the adjustment necessary. Yet watch a golfer on the tee. There he stands, staring at the flag 400yd away, taking in other objects—the rough, the traps—at other distances. Then, with all these registered, he takes up his stance and begins his waggle . . . two waggles and he looks up at the flag . . . two more and another look . . . then a series of one waggle and one look culminating in a last snatched glance before going into the back-swing. The range-finder had done its job before he took his stance; perhaps one more look was needed when his feet were fixed, but that is all.

He would not forget what his first look had conveyed, but

he strains the range-finder several times more and the last, worst of all, just before the shot. He has confused the focus by a factor varying according to the condition of his eyesight and to other factors of optics including the subtle colour influence arising from the difference between the shade of the tree, probably green, and the colour scheme ahead. The eye's reaction to colour changes is a fact of physiology; it is not instantaneous and is no aid to focus. If you give the range-finder a simple picture for its estimation and time to adjust it will signal the brain a clearer image, and the imprint upon the psyche will be correspondingly favourable.

All your strength and muscular co-ordination will be concentrated subconsciously and your mind will be void of the distractions of trying to remember this or that hint or detail of your drill. You will make a good shot. I would say that you will stand a better chance of making a better shot. Certainly, anyone who has driven on a motorway will understand the problem of changing focus. The service-station bun may be brittle, but it is not blurred.

I plead guilty to both charges. Not only have I looked repeatedly but I have waggled without thinking and would like other offences—manifold sins and wickednesses against the peace of swinging harmony—to be taken into account too. The question is, Why does one do these things?

The answer is surely that one does not feel right. There are knots in the nervous system controlling the muscles. So one has another look to put the problem in broader context, to take the mind off the details in the hope that thereby everything will fall into place in supercharged repose. The theory is in line with Sir John's; the practice, conducted by golfing rabbits in a frenzy of fidgeting haste, happens to put the ball out of focus. It need not be so. The masters employ the same principles, but they do not look and waggle because they are confident of the mechanics of their game and are quickly comfortable in their stance. If they are not, or are distracted, they step away and start again. Masters give themselves time and take little; others give themselves none and take longer.

I have often watched with envious astonishment the lack

of fuss in a professional's shot-making. It almost seems careless, but, with confidence such as his in his striking, his problem is different and broader. Once he has assessed it in his approach to the ball and worked out the requirements for conveying it from where it is to where he wants it to be, he can forget the stage. The computer of his brain has decreed the means; the mechanical swing will carry them through. There is no gain in beating about the bush—which is where I always seem to be.

A Fox Takes a Golf Ball

SIR,

On Tuesday, 20 November, the deputy director, Royal Naval Staff Course, Greenwich, the Commandant, RAF Staff College, Bracknell, and the Commandant of the Staff College were playing the ninth hole of a three-ball game at Camberley Heath as part of the triangular golf match celebrating our Joint Winter Training Period. The Navy's ball was some 30 yards from the green, and we were 40 yards away, when out of the bushes on the left trotted a full-grown dog fox, who picked up the ball and returned to cover. Captain Edwards seized a club (a seven iron, I believe) and galloped after him shouting 'Avast' and 'Belay'; Reynard dropped the ball, by now damaged beyond use, and made off.

P. J. HOWARD-DOBSON (Major-General)
Staff College, Camberley, Surrey

Man and Boot

Some notes in admiration of the footwear which denotes enterprises of pith and consequence

LITTLE LESS THAN LOVE LINKS A MAN WITH HIS BOOTS. THE very word opens up horizons of endeavour and achievement. Mention boots and visions grow. The virile monosyllable strikes different chords from the grey and insipid nouns designating other footwear. Memories of my various boots leave me looking back across the vista of the years, thankful for good times, hard times, and good friends in whose company they were worn. As I look forward across the unexpended portion of the same vista, the boots I have yet to wear summarise ambitions for the future; more mountains to climb, more horses to ride, more rivers to wade. The prospect puts me under starter's orders for a race with that old fugitive Time to do it all before too late.

Win or lose, boots already have me in their debt. From slippered ease I salute them. They have helped me through days of gold and iron. Far away now is the portentous day when first my legs slid into hunting boots. In the shop, surrounded by silver-haired men with the prestige of Harley Street surgeons, it had seemed improbable that instep and ankle could take the tight turn leading into the foot. But they did. The silver-haired men knew their craft. In the saddle afterwards there had been that unbelievable thing, the instant marriage of leather to leather. Boot and flap had come together and stayed together as if by magnetic force. My thanks have gone out for this reassuring union on many a cold morning when a horse had his back up.

My fishing boots in winter hang upside-down stuffed with newspaper, a habitation for earwigs. In Spring they herald the new season. Where next?

Shooting boots are not what they were. To write this both grieves and pleases me. The thoroughbred leather version, worn below well-scrubbed spats, has gone out of my life. In their place has come rubber. The transition has not been without misgiving. Sometimes, pulling on the bland green comfortable, watertight, insulated, inexpensive newcomers, I wonder if I should resign from my club. To wear anything which does not require neatsfoot oil and dubbin negates a

ritual of the shooter's life. Rehabilitation of boots formerly ranked second only to the cleaning of guns. Now they are merely held under a tap. This does not seem right.

Many of us wore boots when nothing came easily. To a soldier it seems strange that the largest and most flamboyant boots of World War II were worn by airmen. They fought seated. My boots, officer's, marching, gave up the ghost while

I was yet hale and hearty. Thereafter it was boots, ammunition, for me. I and my first pair reached the end of our tether together.

The road leading from disaster repeated itself for weeks on end. Endlessly it led up into the invisibility of cloud; endlessly it led down into the invisibility of mist. The enemy had broken contact. There was no view in Asia to challenge that of one's own feet. To see them involved no loss of energy in lifting one's head. Endlessly one foot replaced the other, squirting up the khaki dust so that we seemed to march through knee-high smoke. Endlessly the uppers opened and closed on the protruding nails of the soles, like the jaws of two faintly snapping crocodiles. I had other pairs for the march back. They never won my heart as did the old wrecks which brought me out.

In these better times moments still come which are not very different. Down to a valley road after a climb, boots come off and shoes go on for the walk back to the hotel. Not for me alone, perhaps, that flash of communion with the tricorns on which our lives depend. Smoothed and polished by duty and endurance, they earn a glance of gratitude before they are stowed in the pack.

Boots have a voice, too, in urgency or ease. The rhythmic manly multiplied beat of those same ammunition boots comes to hard-pressed men as the sound of hope fulfilled when another company moves in. The crunch of boots on gravel, with an undertone of soft Highland talk as ghillies gather, is the best of overtures to a Scottish day.

Let the angels write me as a man of boots. There are many such, and we are a distinctive community when compared with those less solidly shod; for us the pleasant rigours, for them the dexterities of life. Providence gave me neither skill at games, nor interest in them, except to find an alibi for not playing them. But should all alibi fail I would parade with the cricketers, footballers and boxers, booted as they are, rather than with the golfers, tennis players and bowlers who tread their primrose paths in shoes.

23

The Art of the Walking Stick

The first essential is plenty of time in the search for a lifelong companion

FINDING A SHANK IS AN ESSENTIAL PRELIMINARY TO THE ART OF stick or crook making. It requires almost as much care as shaping and polishing the walker's companion. Quiet corners where hazel, ash and holly grow are not so plentiful as formerly, but can be found for the seeking in most parts. The next essential is permission to cut, though this should need no reminder. A request is seldom refused. I was seeking sticks on a nearby farm when a local landowner rode by. 'You will not find many here,' he said. 'Go to Ellemire Banks.' 'Whom do I ask?' 'Me!' The kind invitation led to a stick-hunting expedition next day.

Ellemire abounds in coppice hazel, ground ash and holly, with blackthorn-lined hedges and various willows for the experimenter. Pheasants and the occasional rabbit showed the sporting instincts of the owner, and a woodcock soared overhead as I approached. Stick cutting demands leisure. It should not be attempted in a hurry or as a burden. To plan to cut a score of sticks an hours is futile. As the Duke of Illyria said in *Twelfth Night*, 'these most brisk and giddy-placed times' have no part in stick making. The hazel growing straight and true may be part of a large clump, and if the root is needed to form the head, considerable digging and cutting are called for.

Tools for stick cutting include a handy spit, preferably with narrow blade as favoured by rabbiting men. An axe of medium weight, and a small selection of saws, complete the kit. My favoured hazel entailed digging around the root-stock until the required part could be sawn down with a Bushman. Unwanted root was then trimmed to reduce weight, always bearing in mind that the stick dresser, like the hairdresser, can remove but cannot replace. A fine one-piece stick may be made from a straight stem growing upwards from one of the hazel's trunks. These often incline from the vertical, so that the proposed shank leaves the main stem at an angle.

The first cut on the latter should be a foot or more above the junction; if one saws the exact place to form the stick head, there is serious danger that the stem will splinter and render the piece useless. Once safely on the ground it may be trimmed more exactly. This initial rough shaping helps drying out, an essential stick-making process. Sticks should dry for two or preferably three years before carving and polishing. Rapid drying must be avoided, and an uninsulated concrete floor is ideal on which to stand blocks.

Those seeking shanks for a horn or a separate wood head have a slightly easier task. They are not concerned with root or block, only with a straight shank of uniform thickness and pleasing appearance. A tapered stick will never balance properly in the hand. These shanks should be bound tightly round a straight, thicker centre pole, and hung up to dry in bundles of a dozen. Thumb sticks take time in the finding. More popular in England than in Scotland, they consist of a straight shank ending in a V formed by two small branches. 'Seek and ye shall find', but the seeker of the perfect thumb stick must have perseverance. The search is no penury. Sticks should be cut when the sap is low, but there is no time like the present if one finds the stick of one's dreams before someone else does. Blocks may be placed in running water to remove sap. If during the winter the plan is to make six sticks, at least a score of shanks is needed and preferably more. The shank may then be matched exactly to the head. Although hazel proliferates so widely there is no reason for wasting nature's reserves and a well-balanced stick will be a joy for ever.

Ever-open Doors

Gone are the days when the Englishman's home was his castle, and all were free to enter at will

WHEN WE GO AWAY MY WIFE LEAVES A NOTE FOR THE burglars. It says that the silver is in the bank, and so are unspecified valuables. Her purpose is to save industrious fellows the toil and sweat of wrecking the place in search of what is no longer there. This pre-departure rite has my admiration. To see in one's partner such fidelity to detail, not to say consideration for others, makes glad the heart of man. Yet for long it seemed a belt-and-braces operation. Now my opinion is modified.

An excessive luminance on the inner door of the porch greeted me on two mornings this summer. I am habitually first down. The brightness of the frosted glass had only one explanation. The outer door had been left open and the light of a new day was shining through. Since the silver was present and burglars absent on each occasion no harm had been done. This was special relief since the door could have been left open only by me. I am habitually last up. Nevertheless, my mind had its forebodings.

The significance of this mild anxiety eventually dawned upon me. What was remarkable was that it should be felt at all. In the 1950s nobody bolted doors, and seldom even closed them from May to September, in my home village. Day and night they stood open. Nobody worried. Nobody intruded. Nobody stole. Such was then the climate of life in the English countryside. We assumed that not only our neighbours, but all who might come and go, were honest. Experience did not prove us wrong. To have locked a door would have implied otherwise, made us feel uncomfortable, and left us wondering against whom we turned the key.

26

The open door was the symbol and result of faith in each other. It was also the channel of communication. How else would the sexton retrieve the key to the belfry from the rectory cloakroom? Or the Calor gas man change the cylinders? Or the postman pick up the outgoing letters? Or the gardener water the conservatory plants? An Englishman's home was and is his castle. But defence was unnecessary as recently as that. Things are changed. Keys and bolts are needed now. Perhaps moat and portcullis, or their equivalents, will be needed next. But let us hope not. And I believe not. Incontrovertibly we were recently a great people. No doubt assails me that we still are, though the evidence has been submerged for lack of familiar outlets for our qualities. Among the things which made us great was team spirit. We were Britons, and aware of what this meant. 'Come the four corners of the world against us' was not an empty phrase. Its legacy permeated everyday life. Those who live thus do not steal from comrades. More of us felt comradeship then than feel it now.

It was our habit then to think of our united interests. What benefitted Britain would in the end benefit all. It had not become fashionable to stress, and if necessary create, fission between sections of the people. Honesty was a national asset, and anything else was unworthy of us. Since then the crime rate has soared. One day we British will exercise our commonsense, which though latent, never fails. Then we shall cease listening to the muddleheads who pretend that larceny is a social evil for which those who do not steal are in some way as much to blame as those who do. Instead we shall recognise again the old good habits which enabled us to live happily together with ever-open doors.

Salmon amid Snow and Ice

A fisherman tells of the rigours and rewards on Scottish rivers when the year is young

THOSE OF US WHO MAKE A HABIT OF GOING OUT AFTER SPRING salmon in Scottish rivers often spend some of our early days each season among snow and ice. Such days are not perhaps the most enjoyable, trying to cope with slippery banks and frozen lines with feet and hands devoid of feeling. There is, however, a kind of fierce satisfaction in it all and, when the first silver-and-blue springer is laid on the snow to be admired, the cold is forgotten and it is all worth-while.

Because of the low temperatures, spinning is the usual method of tempting the fish. They are inclined to be lethargic and will not chase after a spinner in such conditions as they may do in warmer times. Slow spinning, and well below the surface with the spinner, is the angler's aim. It used to be said that the spinner had to be bumping on the bottom to be successful in the cold. As a young man I followed that advice for several seasons, but I caught few fish and left a trail of snagged spinners behind me.

From many hours spent watching salmon, I feel that the normal fish likes to take in an upward, curving movement so that a lure passing slightly above the lie is more likely to tempt the fish than is one down on a level with the salmon's head. My best catches of spring salmon have been taken on the fly. Even when snow has covered the banks, constant streams of ice floes drifting down the river and played fish having to be sledged ashore across marginal ice, the big, heavy fly has brought me as many as six salmon in the short, early day on many occasions. The spinner has never done that for me. I well remember one day on Tweed when snow was not only lying everywhere but also falling heavily as I fished.

Until about 11 o'clock I cast a 3in tube fly into the black water with no success. Then I decided to try putting on a second tube, giving me a lure about six inches in length.

Almost at once the big lure was taken and I landed my first fish. By one o'clock I had six springers on the bank. And each one of the fish was hooked so securely that scissors had to be used to remove the iron. I have tried the double tube since then with occasional reward, but never to the extent of that first time. Of course, the fact that the fish seemed to

go mad for the big lure that day proves little except, perhaps, the unpredictability of the salmon. Had I continued to fish with the single tube I might well have caught the fish just the same. One day on the Tay in early April, when snow showers were sweeping down the valley, the ghillies were harling while I was casting a big Silver Wilkinson from the bank. None of us did any good, but a man fishing for trout hooked the only salmon on a number 12 Black Gnat.

It intrigues me to think about how one can often do well among the salmon when severe wintry weather is over the land, yet when the slightest air of frost comes down in the evening of an early summer day, as often happens in Scotland, that slight chill almost invariably puts the fish down completely. The old idea that salmon will not rise when the air is colder than the water holds good, in my experience, only in such circumstances when the drop in air temperature comes on rather suddenly after hours of relatively warm conditions. One does not need a thermometer to check when the line is freezing but the water is not ice-bound. And many times I have taken fish in such conditions. Indeed, there have been times when I have had to immerse my rod in the running water, while playing a fish, to clear the rings of ice. This, of course, is only a temporary remedy but it does work.

When water rises suddenly, as happens on hydro-electric controlled waters, fish may take during the first few minutes of the increased flow but, thereafter, they go off for perhaps one or even two hours before apparently settling to the new water conditions. It might be, therefore, that in the chill of the summer evening such a time lapse would see them rising again, but since the chill is usually just before sunset, the light has gone before one can test this out.

I believe that light has much to do with salmon's reactions to lures. And the dark, overcast skies that in snow conditions make the water look black, give a light that seems to be ideal for fish to take. Could it be that the dark, dull light can make the fish move regardless of temperature? Generally we find that the metallic light which so often reflects from the water surface in summer is there when the sun goes low in the evening. And that hard light very seldom gives us good fishing in any temperature.

We can only keep casting despite our theories, and hope that the unpredictability of the salmon may, in the worst of conditions, bring us a fish.

Pin-up Before Dinner

*A slight case of line-shooting by a guest who found his hostess
facing a crisis*

IT PUZZLES ME THAT MEN WHO CAN SADDLE A HORSE AND
whelp a bitch should make such an unconscionable song and
dance about putting a nappie on a baby. Yet many do. To
hear their comments one might suppose the infant to be a
malevolent carnivore, or radio-active. Without pride, since
none is justified, I record that this useful and frequent operation is within my power to perform. I performed it the other
night, when our hostess (who, like many hostesses, was performing the last rites in the kitchen) heard wails from
above. She sensibly announced the necessity and impossibility of being in two places at once, and waited for something to happen.

Never volunteer for anything is a sound military maxim
which Napoleon unaccountably failed to include among his
eight principles of war. I nevertheless volunteered this time.
Our host, dispensing drinks, found increasing calls upon his
attention. The ladies, chattering like starlings over the gin-
and-French, raised their conversation a decibel or two by
way of signifying that they had not heard.

It was not difficult. At six months old the young person did
not require a double arm lock to keep her quiet. In the
manner of her kind, she welcomed the attentions of a male
even if it was, so to speak, a blind date. Her mother was
better pleased than she will be about blind dates 15 years
hence. 'Passable,' she said, when inspecting the job.

It was fair comment. A conscientious craftsman does not
relish over-praise, and my nappie-rating is workmanlike
rather than artistic. I do the now modish double wrap-over,
two-pin style to which civilisation has advanced from the

31

cruder triangular, one-pin method. But I would not claim that my folds have the smooth interlocking effect of, for instance, Beau Brummel's cravats. But the nappie stays on, and I will warrant my handiwork against leaks. That is as much as any materfamilias should expect from a casual assistant. This one evidently expected even less. 'He's done it,' she announced in tones vibrant with astonishment.

Needless to say, nobody called for a round of cheers. If there is anything certain to lower a man in public esteem it is putting a nappie on a baby. The ladies dismissed the whole business with the chill reserve which is the most daunting thing about women when two or three are gathered together. They contrived to convey, condescendingly, and without saying it, their conviction that the whole business was a lineshoot. The men were equally frosty. They had, it seemed, a maverick in their midst. The side had been let down as surely as if a member of the Holeborer's Union had demeaned himself by knocking in a nail.

Have I heard, the reader asks, that nappies are now outmoded by numerous slip and clip-on plastic and paper substitutes. Yes, I have heard, and very useful they no doubt are for those who live in flats and town houses. But in the countryside we have such rustic appurtenances as washing machines, spin-dryers, sunshine, fresh air, and space for clothes-lines. Here the old order changeth not. For reasons irrelevant to a discussion of general principles, plastic nappies are regarded similarly to plastic horseshoes and Mr Wedgwood Benn—hardly practical propositions.

More central to my theme is surprise, which some may share, at the apparent survival of the idea that helplessness indicates social grandeur. Inactivity in face of an evident need is presumably intended to convey unfamiliarity with what requires to be done. Unfamiliarity, in turn, might indicate assumption that in normal circumstances other hands from behind the green baize door would deal with routine matters. It seldom happens nowadays. Why go on pretending?

Ragwort, Rabbits and Ringworm

The countryside's unholy trinity, and the chain reaction which produces it

RABBITS AND RAGWORT HAVE THIS IN COMMON—BOTH ARE symptoms of poor husbandry. Modern farming has no room for either. Both were associated with the bad old bankrupt era of farming between the wars; and a recent resurgence of both, though happily limited, is a warning against allowing standards to slip.

The one sure way of dealing with an infestation of ragwort is to plough the field and subject it to an appropriate rotation. Ragwort is a biennial which has a poor chance of survival on arable land. The healthy grass of a well-managed ley can also compete with it efficiently. Two or three years of cereal crops followed by a new ley is a sure recipe for tackling the ragwort problem. Unfortunately, there are some ragwort colonies which cannot be eliminated in this way. They are on land which cannot be ploughed, such as steep hillsides or pastures characterised by boulders, bogs or similar obstacles. Here cutting and/or spraying are the usual control methods. Spraying is the better of the two, because ragwort cut and left to lie on the ground becomes palatable to cattle as it wilts, but it is also poisonous.

When growing, ragwort is fortunately unattractive to cattle. Sheep, however, can eat it with impunity, nibbling the plant in its early, roseate stage, in which it spends the first of its two summers. Some farmers have controlled, and perhaps still do control, ragwort by grazing by sheep. In the years of depression thousands of acres of ragwort-infested derelict land were also the home of innumerable rabbits. Now what appears to be a bad ragwort year coincides with an upward trend in the rabbit population. Is this coincidence, or is there a relationship between the two?

Rabbits do not eat ragwort. That fact is perhaps the only real link between the fortunes of the two. For when rabbits abound they will eat almost everything else, including most of the plants which would otherwise compete with the ragwort. When a rabbit colony establishes itself in a new complex of burrows the rabbits first eat the palatable plants immediately outside the entrances. As the supply is exhausted they travel farther afield. Later the distance to be covered becomes so great or the population so increases that they start on the less appetising plants nearer home.

On large areas of chalk downland and sandy heathland in the 1930s the rabbit population reached such a level that grasses were exterminated, leaving little but lichens to cover the thin soil. But ragwort flourished, as did the creeping thistle, another weed unacceptable to rabbits. While ragwort thus owed much to the activities of rabbits, it offered probably only one reciprocal benefit to the animals. It provided cover around the burrow entrances and exits. Rabbits appreciate such cover, and they had destroyed virtually everything else that could supply it. Even bushes and incipient trees had been eliminated by their efficient ring-barking.

It took many years of neglect for farmland to reach this state of impoverishment. Much of the land then reduced to bearing lichen and ragwort is now producing two tons of barley per acre. The improvement has resulted not so much from a campaign to be rid of rabbits and ragwort, but the introduction of efficient farming. Even where the use of the plough, that best of all tools for the purpose, is impracticable, a constructive policy is the most effective. If the land has to be left down to grass, make sure that the ley is a good one, its grasses and clovers stimulated by well-balanced fertilisers. Replace the rabbits by more useful grazing animals.

An old belief connecting ringworm with rabbits may still be widespread. As often happens with these snippets of agricultural lore, it is partly justified. There is, as far as I know, no evidence that rabbits suffer from ringworm or can transmit the disease to other animals, but they *are* connected with the general impoverishment of stock which gives ringworm a chance to spread. Pastures infested with rabbits and ragwort provide poor pickings. Moreover, although the fungus responsible for ringworm is not one of them, numerous parasites and diseases, among them roundworms, liver flukes and ticks, harboured by rabbits, can be passed on to cattle.

Cattle sharing the meagre herbage between ragwort stalks with thousands of rabbits are therefore likely to be ill-fed and unhealthy specimens, susceptible to ringworm and any other disease with which they come into contact. If they attempt to eke out their diet by eating ragwort they will weaken themselves still further, for ragwort in sufficient quantities can give rise to jaundice, constipation, cirrhosis of the liver and other ills. Despite the fact, therefore, that cattle do not 'catch' ringworm from rabbits or ragwort, observation linking the three rogue 'r's was accurate. It should be added that ringworm can infect healthy cattle as well.

For 2073?

I think that I
shall never see the
branches spreading over me
of that great oak I planted
as a tree for 1973 AD.
Great oaks, they say, from
little acorns grow, and
chestnut trees from chestnuts,
so into the ground I pressed
one; about a week ago.
But if its branches never grow
to shelter me, they may do so
(consoling thought) for those
who follow me; for someone,
say, in 2073.

BERNARD CROFT

35

Village Carnival

Less sophisticated than a fête, freer and easier than a flower show, a good time is had by all

IN A BLAZING SUMMER NOTHING PROSPERS MORE THAN VILLAGE fêtes. The sun shines bright on tents and bunting, strikes sweat from bowlers for pigs, makes tropical the marquees filled with broad beans and flower arrangements, desiccates the gullets of old and young, and flashes back from polished euphonium and pumping trombone. Only we English could have evolved this expression of the joy of living. We are a moderate yet hearty people, so our summer celebration is innocent in character while possessing a certain fervour. Not for us the baring of the soul as in the Eisteddfod of Wales, nor the endurance test of the ceilidhe in Ireland and Western Scotland. In the English manner, our occasions vary from village to village.

Even the titles differ. The generic term fête, perhaps imported long ago from France to lend refinement to occasions which might otherwise have lacked it, is in practice applied to about only one-third of them. The others are equally divided between flower shows and carnivals. In our village it is carnival. Flower shows would be different; not, we think, superior but all very well for those who enjoy them, as we do when neighbouring villages organise theirs. At flower shows peers and baronets wear panama hats, farm men shirts of spotless white, ladies of distinction make opening speeches, and tea is served on something other than a come-and-get-it basis. Such things do not happen at our carnival. But much else does.

It lives up to its name. It magnetises family parties far and wide. Our sense of propriety is not dead. But we have learned to call upon it only in rare cases of excess, as when the

36

rector's bicycle greeted the next dawn on top of my apple tree and opinion was unanimous and instant that 'them roughs from up the valley' had put it there.

We begin exhilaratingly with a procession through the village, tractors towing 'decorated' trailers. The adjective is interpreted in a sense well wide of decorum. In our garden overlooking the carnival field, that which is to come steals

upon the ear long before it meets the eye. First, the thump and blaring of the band; then the plaudits, laughter and wolf-whistles of the multitude. Abandon now any idea that inhibitions linger in the countryside. Mardi Gras and Jagar Nath can take a tip from Wessex in July.

We no longer scour the country for an opener. It will be a sad day when the village itself cannot provide one. All we ask is that she be nubile and possess the spirit and determination to make herself heard above extempore witticisms. She need only call attention to the self-evident fact that the carnival is now well and truly open, that prizes are to be won, and that feasting may begin on cakes and ale, pork pies and tea, ginger pop and candyfloss and other sustaining nourishment.

The conventions are as strict as anywhere. Not a necktie is to be seen; in fine weather, few shirts either. Ladies who sit admit to being over seventy. Men seen in the tea tent are letting their side down. Adolescents segregate the sexes as they march and counter-march. Experienced eyes see signs that thoughts are stirring. Children flock and chirrup like young sparrows.

Strange and stirring sights abound. Young men with long hair and huge muscles perform prodigies with prong and bale, the gamekeeper easily wins the bending race for Land-Rovers in reverse, there are awesome strivings in the tug-of-war, a talented and buxom lass wins the trampoline-somersault contest without relinquishing her ham sandwich (a detail which escapes the attention of some connoisseurs).

Suddenly, though hours have passed, it is time for the year's great classic, the young wives' sack race. This is more than a contest of skill and daring. It forewarns the suspension of levity. As the blushing matrons bite the dust across the finishing line the bandsmen are emerging from the places of refreshment and forming up. Nobody needs telling what to do. Silence hushes festivity. Bleating sheep can be heard again and a passing bee. Parents and children stand in little groups of arrested motion for *Abide with me*. There is a shuffle as men come to attention and the few hats present come off for 'the Queen'. We end always with Retreat.

End? Not exactly. Bacchanalia, if not Saturnalia, will follow. The primeval modern dancing rhythms in the village hall should be enough to rouse the ghosts of the Vikings who once dwelt here and set them reaching for their drinking horns and mead. This is England, and they began it.

The Craft of the Hoe

For and against the use of the virtuous gardener's stand-by

THERE ONCE APPEARED A GARDENING ARTICLE BY A LADY WHO castigated all those who were for ever 'poking and prodding' with a hoe. Hardly has one turned one's back on that immaculate soil before it is scruffy again with weeds that have sprung up from legions of disturbed seeds. Let sleeping seeds lie might have been her motto, and a sensible one too. Nevertheless, there is a time and a place for most things gardeners do, and I am glad I did not follow my first impulse on reading that article, which was to present my Dutch hoe to someone whose dedication to the dust mulch was absolute.

Most of my horticultural life has been spent in fruit, and I have lived long enough to know that in the first year or two of a soft fruit garden the Dutch hoe is truly the gardener's assistant if it is handled properly. If handled wrongly and plied round the bases of the bushes or canes it can wreak havoc, but that is not the fault of the hoe.

No matter how well the ground is prepared, and such preparation is essential for soft fruit, weeds will spring up the next season, perhaps because of all that digging and delving. Many of them may be no more than chickweed, groundsel and the like, though on most soils there will be seedling docks and fat hen; on sandy soils there will usually be thistles, nettles, and perhaps dock seedlings in multitudes.

There is much evidence from experimental work to prove that even a weed cover of annuals, let alone one of rampaging perennials, will use enough water to check severely the growth of young fruit plants in a season when rainfall is light and soil moisture at a premium. Hoeing may beget weeds, but weeds will grow whether we hoe or not. In dry summers they will use soil moisture that should go to the young fruit plants, and in wet summers they are primary sources of greymould, to which raspberries and strawberries are particularly prone. The sensible policy is to hoe them off before they have become sufficiently established to present these hazards. The ideal weed control on ground that has been well cleaned at the start is the mulch that is spread thickly over the entire root area of the bushes, but this would often mean more compost than most people could spare. The compromise is to mulch the plants, preferably in continuous strips, about 18in wide for raspberries, and at least 2ft for bush fruit, and to keep the alleyways hoed up to the end of August.

From autumn until early spring weeds in the alleyways will do no harm, and in wet autumns will do considerable good. If they take moisture from the fruit bushes, so much the better, because we do not want growth from these at the end of summer. What we want is ripe wood, and we are more likely to get this if the plants are on the dry side at that time of year. Soil hoed weed free late in the season looks clean and tidy and all ready for the frost, but what does it look like in spring when the winter rains have rained upon it? It is caked and puddled, or scored with erosion channels if it slopes, and frost will have done little more than create cracks in the surface. But if it had a cover of vegetation it will be nicely friable by March and amenable to the Dutch hoe.

There can be a substantial difference in growth rate and general establishment of first-year soft fruit bushes that were clean cultivated throughout summer, as opposed to those that suffered competition from weeds. The initial season is the testing time, especially for raspberries and black currants, which are not only becoming established but are also making wood for cropping in its second year. A well-grown black currant bush will have at least five strong shoots, often six or seven, by the season's end, if the stock was good; one that went thirsty, and therefore hungry as well, will have weak, spindly shoots that may have to be cut right back to give the bush a second chance. Thus a year will be lost, and if we jib at cutting back and leave the bushes to crop, the yield will be poor, but the strain of producing it will often weaken the bush still further.

Where fruit trees are planted straight into grass they can suffer crippling competition unless measures are taken to reduce this at the beginning and are maintained until the trees are established. But modern research has shown that competition is not so drastic as it was once thought to be if efficient grass cutting goes with mulching. Grass should be cut each time it reaches about 4in in height, and the cuttings should never be carted off but should be left to rot. If there is not enough material for the mulching, then clean rings of soil some 4ft in diameter should be left round each tree. Even where a tree is planted in a lawn—in which case it will usually be a half or full standard—it will still suffer competition; this is undoubtedly the reason, or the basic reason, why so many lawn-planted fruit trees take years to get going, or sometimes never get going, but remain small or stunted.

Primrose Wood

> *I wandered in a primrose wood,*
> *   The soft leaf-mould was sweet with Spring,*
> *I leant against a blackthorn tree,*
> *   And heard birds sing.*
>
> *I picked a bunch of dawn-pale flowers,*
> *   Then suddenly the birds were still,*
> *The sky grew darker and I heard*
> *   Thunder—beyond the hill.*
>
> *Swiftly and sharply came the rain,*
> *   Like silver spear among the thorn,*
> *Then sunlight shone, birds sang again,*
> *   And Spring was born. . . .*

M. H. HUNT

Mourning the Moustache

A lament for the decline of the handle-bar, soup-strainer, walrus and the rest

UNDER THE FORTHRIGHT GAZE OF SOME RARELY SEEN ANCEStral portraits my thoughts turned to a national decadence. They concerned the sorry state which now afflicts that once inspiring feature, the British moustache. In its former richness and diversity it typified a virile nation. But now . . .?

Many of my fellow citizens have become content to resemble consumptive apaches. Their drooping, ill-kempt, supra-labial hair turns inward and downward at the corners of the mouth. The effect is a gaunt, devitalised, half-starving impression. Others favour beards which are allowed to rampage untrimmed. These bestow on their proprietors a weak, defensive air, as of men for ever peering apologetically over blackthorn hedges. Failures in beardmanship, however, may be passed over lightly. Unlike the moustache, the beard is not a feature deeply entrenched in the British way of life. Seafarers alone have taken to it unselfconsciously. Even there, doubt obscures the motivation. Perhaps it is for warmth, and thus even more necessary now that grog has been discontinued. Perhaps it is mere lack of dexterity with the razor in ships rolling and pitching across the storm-lashed oceans. Except among the few enthusiasts the beard can hardly be regarded as an art form. The moustache certainly is one. To arrest its decadence, the Ministry of the Environment should step in.

To consider, as I did, the faces of past generations is to mourn what we have lost. Where now can be seen the baroque rhythms of Dundreary whiskers in combination with unshaven lip but shaven chin? The pressures of modern life preclude such time-consuming cultivations. More is the pity.

In addition to much else, we owe the Royal Air Force

gratitude for a brief renaissance in moustache development during World War II. Their officers reintroduced that hall-mark of masculinity, the handlebar. Many such moustaches achieved impressive spans, sweeping to port and starboard like the horns of a buffalo. Not every man can carry off the handlebar effect as to the manner born, any more than every man can fly aircraft in battle. Both demand buoyancy of spirit, and attention to detail. Much brushing is needed to obtain lustre, since the handlebar must be couth, without loss of droop resistance. Only the dedicated attempt it, and dedication is rare.

Rather less demanding was the cavalry. This was slightly shorter in the beam, and brushed upward at the extremities. The effect was to add a dash of arrogance to the manly virtues conferred by the handlebar.

The rural scene especially has been poorer for the obsolescence of the erstwhile badge of squirearchy, the soup-strainer. A genuine specimen is now rare. It was invaluable in conferring at least a temporary impression of respectability and prudence even when these qualities were lacking. It was another marque which could not be worn without due care and attention. Contrary to the implications of its name, it was more hindrance than help when eating or drinking, and led to the redesign of table ware. Tea cups were made with a gridded section which kept the moustache out of harm's way while its owner refreshed himself. Lack of the device was apt to lead a soup-strainer to lose its pristine gloss and symmetry, and to degenerate into the next best thing, the walrus. Much that was endearing attached to this mode, still sported today by bluff old colonels and the like. But in the golden age when moustaches were more than mere accidents of Nature, the walrus was held to indicate a moustache owner who had seen his best days.

Its antonym was the tooth-brush. This satisfied humanity's ever-present craze for bantamisation. So far from seeking to enhance their moustaches, its devotees behaved like ladies with chihuahuas, vying to produce a smaller one.

Civilian Britain never had much use for wax. Not so the Army of yesteryear. Warrant officers laboured to produce projections like poignards on either side of the face, presumably in the belief that this would enhance their reputations for ferocity and prestige. A similar faith in waxed points pervaded the Balkans (the world's great forcing ground of moustache evolution) until a generation ago. Few reputable bandits or political agitators would have deigned to earn their daily bread unless so adorned.

My own contribution to our own gross national moustache-product is unspectacular. It reflects my disposition—unobtrusive, neat but not gaudy. In this the evidence of those ancestral portraits suggests a genetic reversal. For they, in the fine flowering and infinite variety of their natural embellishments, could not be so lightly dismissed.

Ode to Alban

But few scant roods of Alban do I own
By wax-sealed testament or title deed;
   The sight of her fair face, and that alone
Is all the real estate I'll ever need.
   Yet mine are all her lovely haughs and hills
From Taymouth's tilth to wilds beyond Loch Fyne.
For love, not grudging last-hour codicils,
Have made these proud possessions truly mine.
   Each heathery knoll and every birchen bower,
The darkling corrie where the eagles nest,
All, all were mine for one enchanted hour.
Alban belongs to him who loves her best.
And so to bed, for in my Land of Dreams,
Bent backs are straight and weary hearts are young;
   Alban still smiles on me, or so it seems,
The final song of rapture's still unsung.

JACK FRY

44

Lookers on the Marsh

How the freelance shepherds of Kent and Sussex maintain their ancient independence

SO FAR AS I HAVE BEEN ABLE TO ASCERTAIN, THE TERM 'LOOKER' —as used to describe a self-employed shepherd of the Kent and Sussex marsh country—is peculiar to this corner of England. Where might you spot a typical looker? For less than £1, one could board a mid-morning, three-coach train from platform No 4 at Ashford (Kent) railway station. It passes with frequent, pleasing halts, through Ham Street and Orlestone, Appledore, Rye, Winchelsea and on to old Hastings town. As one travels, to the right is the great sweep of the Marsh towards the hogsback of land-locked Oxney Isle, to Wittersham and distant Tenterden. To the left and coastwards, one can see across the vast Walland Marsh, to Romney, Brenzett, Lydd and Camber.

There, the lookers, heads bent into the wind, eager, loping dogs at heel, plod the edges of the shimmering dykes that divide those world-famous, evergreen, billiard-table pastures —close-clipped by perhaps the greatest single concentration of ewes and lambs that a man's eyes can span in a wide glance. Whether lookers are truly shepherds is a most delicate and controversial issue. Many an old Marsh flockmaster would insist there was a subtle difference between the two. Others, equally experienced, would disagree. Lookers themselves, almost without exception, would argue that there are few, if any, duties that a 'shepherd' does better than a good 'looker'. Shepherds hint that a looker is not a shepherd but a looker. It is difficult to get farther than that. The marsh-land is full of subtleties and sidestreams of thought.

Perhaps the main difference, and the one which may explain a lot, is that the looker customarily serves more than

45

one master at the same time. 'Lookering' is an ancient skill. The old-time lookers were, as I see it, the forerunners of our modern contract-shepherds. Lookering runs in marsh families and its skills, wrinkles and the intense personal knowledge of farms and grazings are passed from father to son with ritual secrecy.

The old lookers of the south-eastern marshes rode about their business on ponies. Lookers usually preferred to use their own tools and medicaments, including perhaps a 'dead cart'—a small, two-wheel trolley suitable for a wide range of short-haul jobs, including the removal of carcasses. Now a van or Land-Rover transports them from one site to another.

They were, and some might say still are, a fiercely-independent, tight-tongued race of men, proud of their self-employed status and the choice of employers it conferred. For a price agreed with the flockmaster, the looker undertook the lookering on all the farmer's lands, carrying out a multiplicity of tasks connected with pasture and sheep management. Most lookers chose to be 'acre-lookers', they contracted to look after all the sheep grazing an acre of marsh, rather than work on a headage basis.

A farmer had a wide choice of services. The charge for the most basic duties of lookering, just prior to the First World War, was around 1s 6d per acre per year. Additional fees were struck for the various 'one off' shepherding tasks—shearing, 'footing', dagging, dosing and droving. In 1912, a looker would receive 2s 9d for hand-shearing each score of adult sheep and 2s 6d per score of lambs. Men like Bill Marshall, William Adams and George Chittenden—famous Romney Marsh lookers—could shear 100 sheep a day, working to punctual hours of stop and start, and using hand shears.

Marsh lookers built huts for shelter and the storage of equipment, away out on the wind-swept 'levels'. There was a code of conduct whereby a looker faced with an emergency could hoist a flag above his hut. His nearest colleague, after giving his own sheep a final glance, would set off across the lonely marsh to give aid. A grim tale of the 1880s is told of a 'pikey', or wandering itinerant who, when tramping the Romney Marsh, gleaning wool from the fences, was overtaken by a terrifying storm of thunder and rain. He saw in the distance a looker's hut and struggled on to reach it. The storm had abated by the time he found the refuge, to discover a young looker boy, ashen-faced, sobbing and bewildered, standing outside. 'Look at me,' whined the pikey. 'Look what a dreadful state I am in. Let me come in to dry myself.' 'Things here are in a dreadful state, too,' whispered the boy. 'Come inside.' And inside the hut sat five lookers, inert, staring unblinkingly from the gloom. All had been struck dead by lightning.

The legendary link between marsh lookers and smuggling is not without some certain, if small foundation. Bill Booth, 44 years a shepherd at Court Lodge, Lyminge, high on the downs above the Romney Marsh, tells a true story of his grandfather, William Booth, an acre-looker born in the Isle of Oxney. William Booth swam, on a winter's night, up the River Rother with three one-gallon kegs of brandy attached by a line to his person. Mounted preventive officers were patrolling the banks and Booth-of-Oxney was forced to hide for a long time in the frosted reeds until the coast was clear. Bill himself, now in his seventies and one of East Kent's most respected shepherds, is descended from a famous family of marsh lookers. He left New Romney School in 1912 to become 'looker boy' to his looker father and, apart from Army service in World War I, has been shepherding ever since.

When, today, we see the huge, sophisticated livestock transporter vehicles strumming along the highways crammed with sheep, it is hard to understand that, no so long ago, many such journeys had to be undertaken on 'Shanks's pony'. In the September and March of each year, Bill Booth and others like him, would begin their great treks, driving thousands of sheep and lambs from one county to the next. Romney Marsh lambs would be driven in Autumn to Winter keep in West Sussex and Surrey and back again in Spring. Bill's biggest drive was 2,496 sheep from East Grinstead to the Marsh in the spring of 1919. The drove extended along the highway for 1½ miles, and was undertaken by six lookers and eight dogs, averaging 10 miles a day. The men would harbour the sheep for the night, board in wayside inns and be on the road again before dawn. The dogs were fed on sheep that 'did not complete the trip'.

Reminders of the past may still be found: 'Lookers House' and 'Lookers Cottage', for instance, on the Pevensey Marsh at the charmingly named Russells-in-the-Marsh. But, in all my travels in the marsh country, I have never come upon a pub called 'The Looker'. If there isn't one, then there should be—to honour the old calling.

In at the Kill

*A moment of truth for a small girl and a moment of enlighten-
ment for her father*

THE WIND THAT TOSSED THE TREES ABOUT DID NOT MOVE THE
kestrel. On lifted wings and downthrust tail he hovered as
steady as a weathercock, the one fixed point on an April day
when young corn waved and shone like a flowing tide. He
was 30 yards from us. I showed him to my daughter.

'He can fly standing still,' she sang out. Ladies aged six
seldom moderate their voices. 'Why is he?'

She listened to my summary. He was trying to catch something to eat. Whatever it was, perhaps a mouse, was in the
stubble. He was watching it, waiting to drop on it.

'Where is it?' came in piercing tones. 'I want to see.'

Like a man when he is fishing, the kestrel was immune to
the human voice. He was in a closed world of wind and
stubble, containing only himself and his quarry. His concentration was absolute, and enviable. We kept moving, not
halting nor hurrying, as if we saw nothing. We were in a
narrow larch belt, windblown over the years. Its battered
pattern gave a little cover without interrupting the view.

The kestrel dipped away then hovered again, now a little
lower and only 20 yards short of a spinney. The downward
tilt of the bluish head was eloquent of urgency and stealth.
'If the mouse gets into the spinney,' I said, 'he'll lose it.'
My daughter jumped up and up. 'Quick, quick, quick,' she
whispered, 'why doesn't he catch it?'

He did. That lethal, exact stoop, seemingly quicker than
gravity's pull on so light a creature, took the kestrel out of
sight into some dead ground. 'He's got it,' I said, and arrested
the would-be eyewitness as she darted forward declaring 'I
want to look'.

D   49

'Wait,' I said. We waited. 'Where is he? What's he doing?' At six years old 30 seconds can seem unreasonable delay. Then, heavily airborne, and not wholly steady on course, the laden kestrel reappeared. The blunt head and short tail hanging from the talons denoted a field vole, plump from the mild winter and gleaning the stubble. Swinging to the wing-beats of the laboured flight, the clean grey underbelly showed. Then came tears. 'Oh, he's killed it,' sobbed a suddenly unconsolable little girl. 'Why did he kill it? Why did you let him? I want a mouse like that to keep.'

So yet another father-daughter relationship faced that particular set of facts which comprise nature in the raw; the food we eat, the things we do, and the things which creatures must do to live. For me it was not the first time. I have been over this line of country twice previously. It is best to point the actualities, and stand by to answer questions honestly. One will end with the impression that the situation could have been better handled, but that is true of most conversations with women. Whether six or sixty, they do not change much.

Without knowing it, a child sees a lifetime's lessons in a glance. This one had learned through the death of the vole what the rest of us feel at the end of every hunt, the empti-ness which comes when a fox is rolled over, a stag falls to the bullet, or a trout at last makes the fatal misjudgment. It is less sentiment than the swift transition from elation, even triumph, to finality. This reaction could not be explained to a six-year-old. She will learn it, in time. All sportsmen do.

My companion deserted me at the home gate and ran ahead to the house. Her excited communiqué, cut short when a door slammed behind her, closed the episode. 'Mummy, mummy, mummy, we saw a hawk kill a mouse, and he flew away to eat it . . .' She had met her first mixed moment. She had wept, and now she spoke for all sportsmen everywhere.

A Fly-fisher's Master Cast

The story of a Kennet trout caught against the odds is told by a proud father

EACH TIME I PASS A CERTAIN SPOT ON THE KENNET I PAY SILENT tribute to the doer of a mighty deed. It was one of those examples of complete mastery of a difficult situation which resulted in the capture, against long odds, of a specimen trout. Such examples are classics of their kind, sometimes unconventional, sometimes at variance with all accepted theory, and the capture is true art inasmuch as the skill of the angler makes everything look simple. I must own to a certain parental pride in this case, though not, I hope, parental prejudice, for the captor was my son. The catching of that beautiful brown trout, in the pink of condition and weighing a few ounces over 2lb, must rank among the great episodes of the streamside, even though it involved no protracted dramatics, and was all over in less than 60 seconds.

At the place where it occurred the river is about 30yd wide. The trout was right under the far bank, tucked into a small inlet that was overhung by willowherb and long blades of grass. The fly of the moment was medium olive which was hatching from nearby ranunculus. The duns were being carried down on a narrow little current. It skirted the left-hand edge of the bed and flowed between it and the bank, forming a channel that passed a few inches to the left of the trout's nose. In this channel he would turn every so often, take his fly, and then retire the few inches back into his pool. But his movement into the path of the flies was not always a sidelong motion, with his nose upstream; sometimes he would turn sharply, so that for a fraction of time he was looking straight across the river to our bank. Anyone casting directly across, with the object of reducing a long throw to the minimum, would therefore run the risk of being seen if the trout decided to make a sharp turn just when the angler was casting.

My son decided to cast from about 12ft below the fish, which meant a throw of some 31yd. There was no question of a second chance. If the throw was a foot or so too long it would foul the dangling grass, and if it was a foot too short it would land in a weed bed. And that was by no means the only hazard. First, catch your fish. But what do you do with him when the water, almost from bank to bank, is a veritable archipelago of crowfoot beds, a width of water destined for improvement but meanwhile judged unfishable?

I had no idea of what my son's tactics were to be. All I knew was that after we had watched the trout feeding, the problem of catching him seemed to me to be of purely academic interest. Even if he was hooked, he would never be brought through that maze of weedbeds. And I had enough knowledge of those Kennet trout to be pretty sure that if this one did take the fly he would go like a torpedo, and that any attempt to check him would mean disaster. Yet if he was given line he would go straight to weed, for there was nowhere else for him to go. Added to this was the fact that 30 yards is a long way from which to strike a fish.

As we contemplated the proposition, I came to feel that no more than half a victory could be achieved. I was disposed to pass on and seek out a trout in some more likely position, but my son can never resist the long odds chance when it comes to catching trout. So the die was cast. He made two or three false throws for distance, and then landed his medium olive plumb in that narrow little channel; so close to the trout's nose that the take was instantaneous as the fly hit the water. The cast alone was sheer artistry, but the strike and the subsequent operation were of an even higher order.

The vital thing with Kennet trout is to give line freely immediately the fish turns. Any restriction at this moment will almost inevitably mean that the fish will slip off if it is lightly hooked, or will snap the leader if strongly hooked. That was why I had thought the operation doomed to failure, even if the trout was hooked, because there seemed no chance of bringing it to the net if it were given line in that forest of weed. What followed was a demonstration of how theories can be confounded, instincts and convictions turned upside down. I do not think the result could have been achieved except by a perfect combination of the control and lightness of touch that were summed up by Skues in the one word, 'hands'.

My son made no attempt to play the fish. From first to last it was shock tactics, to get his quarry across many yards of weed-infested water and into the net before it had any time to recover from the affront of being hooked. Simultaneously with the turn down of the fish, the rod was raised high to get the trout's chin clear of weed, and the line was pulled through the rings in co-ordination with a short walk downstream, bringing the fish into clear water where he could be netted. I shall always remember the peculiar flapping sound the fish made as it was skated lightly over the weed, and my almost heart-stopping fear that the leader would break. In rough hands it would have broken.

My four fish caught later that evening were fine specimens that gave me a good run for my money, but their capture seemed tame affairs. The highlight had passed; for me there was nothing to bask in but reflected glory.

Butterfly Summer

A touch of the sun on a memory of a schoolboy's first field sport

SPORT'S HIGH MOMENTS HAVE MANY GUISES. A STAG TAKEN IN the labyrinths of wind, a salmon played amid boulders and boiling dubs, a fox hunt seen all through by throwing one's heart over first—the list could be multiplied by every outdoor man. To count blessings is right, and I have been counting mine. They will not be itemised. They are, for a start, private to me. Secondly, nothing is more boring than other men's fish, rights-and-lefts, and lines across country. I cite only a butterfly.

It proved to be a silver-washed fritillary. I had not known this until, with pumping breath and sweat-stung eyes, I examined my trophy in the net. I was nine. The fruit of the tree of knowledge was then incompletely mine. For instance, I realised the rarity of what I had caught. I also knew, for the first time in that moment, that rarity did not matter. Neither did the accolades which would be bestowed upon me by the school natural history society. Nor did the fact that it was 'a good spess' (for specimen). What I had not known until that moment was the full flavour of achievement. The chase had engaged body and soul to the exclusion of mind, and had reached its culmination before the truth dawned. In life's first decade I had learned what sport means. It would have been a pity to wait longer.

If mind had anything to do with it, I should have abandoned pursuit and given the fritillary best. No butterfly could be worth such commitment of physical capability, such disregard of hazard. No pig-sticker crammed into the *jhow* with more contempt for consequence than mine as I hurled myself into head-high, malevolent nettles. Strands of barbed wire, broken bottles, jettisoned machinery could all be expected

in that dumping ground. To hell with them. Where the butterfly flew, I followed. To have done less would have abnegated the manhood yet to come.

So for me, and perhaps for many others, butterfly collecting was the first field sport. We called it bug-hunting in the idiom of the time. The hands of some who read this account will reach for pen and paper to protest at the taking of a rarity. But fritillaries were not rare then. They have become so, along with much else, not because bug-hunters have caught them, but because whole life-forms, plant species and environments have been destroyed by chemicals and cupidity in the pursuit of what self-styled rationalists call progress.

Bug-hunting was not only the first field sport. It is also the basic field sport. It demands and gives back a good measure of all the others. The observation of a fisherman is needed to anticipate what to expect. Nobody can be a bug-hunter without being a botanist too. The fieldcraft of a shooter is crucial. A bug-hunter must make himself part of light and shadow, so as to see and be unseen. Often fieldcraft is enough but, when it is not, there follows, for those young enough, that marvellous thing, a hunt. By that triumph, I knew why my grandfather rode to hounds. Previously I had wondered.

Much stemmed from that fritillary. Several concussions; a shoulder that is the despair of tailors, and sometimes of myself; much exposure to rough weather; days which have ended with skin shrivelled by sunshine; long hours lost in unconsciousness of all but quarry, ground, water, light and wind—hours which Pathans say will be deducted by the Almighty from the expended portion of life's span, as surely as Allah forgives between the stirrup and the ground. Those hours are filled with good companions. Some have been great in their chosen spheres, others poor in substance but rich in spirit. The world of Nature and the disciplines of sport cut us down to size, and elevate us to our proper levels, sometimes simultaneously. For introducing me to them I thank that butterfly.

The cocksfoot was seeding where I lay, flung headlong in the act of capture on that distant summer day. While my heartbeats thudded I watched my fritillary. Unmindful of chase and capture, unconcerned by knowledge of consequence, he opened and closed his bright wings, drinking in sunshine. In my blazer pockets I searched for a specimen box. All were smashed to shavings. An imperial purler in the nettles had done that. So holding the gauze of the net carefully clear of his wings, I walked the fritillary half a mile back to school, and the killing bottle. He sunbathed his way to death. Such unrelenting purpose would fail me now. The grown man would free him but the boy did not waver.

Long years later I opened the cabinet. Ironically, moth had entered. There was no trace of the butterfly, except a labelled pin. In his place he had left me a rich heritage.

The White Admirals

How a small change in human habits may change the world for a wild species (in this case, butterflies again)

THERE IS A THEORY THAT THE SPREAD OF THE WHITE ADMIRAL butterfly through the South of England in the years after the First War was due to the baker delivering bread. Before, the country housewife baked her own bread, and fired her bread oven with hazel which was regularly coppiced for the purpose.

The White Admiral caterpillar feeds on honeysuckle. It hatches from the egg in the autumn and hibernates while still small on its foodplant, relying on its cryptic camouflage for protection against winter predators. This indeed is so good that a man may live in a suitable wood all his life and never see a caterpillar unless he knows what to look for; finding them is a knack that becomes easier with every sighting. Nobody knows how long it takes a cock pheasant to find his first caterpillar, but certainly he soon acquires the knack. While the housewife was baking her bread, the hazel was regularly cut, preventing the honeysuckle from growing higher than a cock pheasant can reach. But when the baker began to deliver, the housewife stopped baking. Down went the demand for firing, up went the hazel, up went the honeysuckle, up went the White Admiral caterpillars out of the cock pheasant's reach, and within a few years the species had spread throughout most of England, south of the Wash. Further advance was prevented probably only by some other factor, perhaps climatic.

Whether this theory is true or not, it is certainly plausible. By such relatively trivial acts man constantly affects the balance of Nature, usually adversely. He drains the fens and puts an end to the Large Copper, of which the British form was the biggest and brightest of all. The Swallowtail, our

57

largest resident butterfly, continues, for the same reason, to exist precariously and only through the efforts of conservationists in maintaining its habitat in restricted localities.

The case of the Whites is slightly different, though the final result is the same. The three common members of this family, the Large, Small and Green-veined Whites, together with the Orange Tip, all feed on plants of the order cruciferae; the first two in particular show a preference for brassica crops. Before the advent of insecticidal sprays, it is probable that the population of these species had been gradually building up in this country over the centuries, due to the activities of man who grew more and more of these vegetables as his own population increased. Now that spraying of commercial crops is a routine matter, the numbers of these butterflies have been cut back sharply. The Green-veined White and Orange Tip, which prefer roadside and meadow plants such as Jack-by-the-Hedge and Cuckoo-pint, perhaps enjoyed less of a build up of population due to man. Likewise, they are less seriously affected today than their cousins, though the spraying and cutting of roadside verges takes a heavy toll.

When people speak, as they so often do, of the present-day shortage of butterflies, they have most prominently in mind the Vanessids. Childhood memories are nearly always of Small Tortoiseshells, Peacocks, Red Admirals, Painted Ladies and (for younger people) Commas in the buddleia and Michaelmas daisies. It is these bright active butterflies which are missed today. Unfortunately, their foodplants are the enemies of man—thistles for the Painted Lady, nettles for the others. Most of them feed gregariously, at least when young, so that a thorough campaign of nettle spraying at the crucial time of year can virtually exterminate butterflies in the area affected.

In the woodlands the story is the same, and the chief offenders are the Forestry Commission. Thirty years ago the rides in the New Forest were edged with brambles, flowering in profusion in the second half of the summer. A bramble bush in August might sport a dozen Silver Washed Fritillaries and half as many White Admirals. In earlier months marsh thistles in the glades were competed for by Dark Green and High Brown Fritillaries, while earlier still the two Pearl Bordered Fritillaries were often in abundance. Now every one of them is much scarcer, and some are becoming rare. The need for efficiency and the desire of the official mind for tidiness have swept away the bramble borders, and even the violets on which the caterpillars of all these species feed cannot exist in the bare black blocks of conifers which extinguish all vegetable life but their own.

Recently the instructions to the Forestry Commission in the New Forest have been amended, and economic efficiency is no longer paramount. Perhaps we shall see a gradual return there of the woodland butterflies. But in other great areas of countryside, both publicly and privately administered, the crop is all-important, and all other living things must be sacrificed for its sake.

Every year at agricultural shows the engineering industry trumpets its success in producing a new improved tractor. The improvements include the ability to plough steeper and rougher slopes. The effect of these improvements on the ground is that here and there a few more acres of downland disappear beneath the plough. Some small areas disappear, others are cut in two.

What are the future prospects for our British butterflies? The voice of the conservationists has never been so strong, but neither has the demand for more houses, more concrete, more home-produced food and timber. Perhaps henceforward the last colony of any one species will be permitted to survive, under strict control and within strict boundaries, but meanwhile the erosion of habitats will continue as long as our islands remain so full of humans.

Guilt and the Seagull

A surprise piece of evidence on those which cause the damage,
and those which do not

WHETHER YOU REGARD THE GULL AS AN EMBLEM OF SPIRITUAL
purity or a down-to-earth scoundrel is likely to depend on
subjective factors. Also, perhaps, it may be on whether it is
viewed high in the sky or at a range where the viewer himself
may be fixed by its cold yellow eye. A hundred years ago,
gulls were shot for sport—of a sort—their eggs taken on a
serious scale for human consumption. This is no longer the
case. Apart from internecine depredations, they suffer but
little natural predation; their growing numbers now begin
to cause concern.

As any professional collector of gulls' eggs would confirm,
to attempt to reduce their numbers by taking their eggs is a
forlorn hope. The robbed gull settles immediately to the task
of proving that it can—at a pinch, so to speak—offer a serious
challenge to Rhode Island Red, Black Leghorn, or what you
will. Confronted by the problem of gull predation on more
highly-valued sea birds, officers on reserves hit on the brilliant idea of contraception by egg puncturing. The gull sits
on the addled egg until too late to resume laying and rear
chicks. Nature reserves, however, accommodate but a tiny
fraction of our gull population; so unless gull-egg pricking
becomes a national pastime, there seems but slight chance
in the immediate future of the population ceasing to grow.
For most of us, this is unlikely to be of deep concern; but to
the man breeding sheep on coastal pastures, the matter has
direct importance.

Recently, I met a man who has bred sheep on Exmoor for
20 years or so on a farm where he also raises cattle and grows
a few acres of arable crops. We had a conversation which

ranged from otters, foxes and the best men he had seen hunt them, to which birds were regarded as true agricultural pests. He gave the blackest character to the great black-backed gull, and was unable to let down much more lightly its lesser black-backed relative. Both were no less a threat to newborn —even week-old—lambs on his farm than fox or carrion crow. Skulls might be punched open, eyes removed, tongues nipped out. No villainy imputed to the greater black-back could ever surprise me and, handsome though the scamp may be, I shed few tears for his destruction.

As we sat in the sturdy stone-built farmhouse, perched on the 900ft contour, it seemed probable that the rogues' gallery described would proceed next to the herring gull. But I was told there was no evidence against this bird. In itself, this was not perhaps so very surprising, but following the strictures against the lesser black-back, it certainly was. So closely related in systematic terms are these two birds that experts are now moving towards a sub-specific rather than separate species relationship for them. It strikes one therefore as distinctly odd that they should, when occupying the same habitat with the same temptations and opportunities, differ in this important respect. The Handbook quotes but a slight variation in examined stomach-contents—98 per cent animal matter for the lesser black-back, 92 per cent for the herring gull, but no mention of lamb killing.

My Exmoor witness struck me as eminently reliable, so my first question is whether the phenomenon is purely local. Whether or not, one ponders deeply on why there should be this apparent anomaly in behaviour. I am brought back to the question of imitativeness. To the systematist, the lesser black-back may be an aberrant herring gull. But does he see himself rather as next of kin to the great black-back, with an inner compulsion to imitate?

To Stand Agostering

The language of the people on Severnside, and its message to an exile in Wessex

EVENING FELL AFTER A LONG WARM DAY. IT BEING SPRING, when there is much to be done, there were warm thirsty men to greet it. They had foregathered at the inn and when time was called they did not at once go home. They stood in the forecourt, gostering. From my garden the sound was clearly audible, spreading its comfortable message to the night that here were talkative and friendly fellows. Coming in from my last rounds, I reported the sound of gostering to my wife. She, reared in the sophisticated atmospheres of the Punjab, Salisbury Plain and Aldershot, did not understand the word. And realisation dawned that I had spoken out of the past.

The verb to goster entered my vocabulary in early youth, from Shropshire. I cannot remember when and where I had last heard it used. But there is no doubt what it means. It refers to that low burble of conversation from cronies enjoying a private chat, erupting periodically into loud masculine laughter which promptly subsides. My grandmother, a serious-minded and purposeful woman, held gostering in disapprobation and spoke of it in withering terms whenever she heard it. To her it signified light-headedness and time-wasting. Additionally her sweetness of disposition never quite overcame the commonly held feminine delusion that when men laugh the motivation is apt to be indelicate.

Knowing better, my memories of gostering are second-hand. To goster at all, one's voice must have broken, and by the time mine had done so we had moved out of gostering country. So it was always as an eavesdropper, never a participant, that I remember those gatherings of shirt-sleeved men in the gloaming at cottage gates or at the tap-room door.

In those days, the first decade after World War I, men gostering on one side of the village could clearly be heard on the other. Not the exact words, of course. The rolling rustic vowels fused together to convey the spirit of what was being said, but hid its exact significance. What mattered was that good human speech was about the loudest sound in the

countryside at dusk. The thunder of aircraft and the revving of cars did not drown it then. The comings and goings of neighbours were signalised by their tones and accents, not by their engine notes. The banalities of television had not mesmerised the community and excluded conversation. So there was much enjoyable gostering on summer evenings, when the day's work was done, especially if the weather was puthery.

That word slipped out unbeckoned in the slipstream of gostering. It, too, came from long ago, and from Shropshire, although I hear my well-travelled mother use it unselfconsciously when occasion demands. Weather becomes puthery when thunder is about, clouds hang low, the air grows heavy with heat and damp, flies swarm, thoughts turn to making cottage cheese, and ale is called for after sundown.

Every county has its own words and phrases. Since most are onomatopoeic and reflect the experiences of ordinary folk, they are among the most expressive in the language. They long had their place as local status symbols. Not to know them was an admission of being an off-comer. Inconvenient as such things can be, my heart warms to dialect. It is a natural manifestation of the independence of Englishmen, of their refusal to conform to a common pattern. Long may they retain this. And of course, dialect was stronger and more important, when, for me, the world was young . . . when roads were dusty, villages self-contained, isolated except on Fair days, and entertainment came from neighbours instead of an electronically fitted box.

It was a good time to be alive. And so is this. Doubtless somewhere, far away from where I write in Wessex, men still goster affably in the Severn vale. Anywhere else, I wonder?

Kings, Saints and Sinners

Not all was polished elegance at Bath in the 1,000 years after England's first Coronation

BATH DOES NOT READILY EVOKE THE AGE OF KING EDGAR. BEAU Nash might be met with on many a street corner without causing much surprise. The brutal simplicities of Anglo-Saxon England are less easy to assimilate amid Georgian sophistication. Even the eye of faith may fail to visualise the Bath of Edgar's day, a town of 25 acres, its thatched and timbered houses huddled within the Roman walls. Still less do the emaciated monks of St Peter's Abbey or St Dunstan, living in a flurry of visions and anathemas, enhance the Palladian calm of the Royal Crescent. Nevertheless, here Edgar was crowned King of All England a thousand years ago on 11 May 973. The ceremony was marked by a splendour which lingered long in the memory of man. As late as 1540, when Leland was travelling England, the townsmen were still wont to elect a King of Bath in honour of the occasion. The ritual which followed at Edgar's crowning laid the foundation of the Coronation ceremony.

All this was achieved only after a misspent youth. Edgar was only 31 when he was buried at Glastonbury, two years after his coronation. He was the great-great-grandson of King Alfred and succeeded in 959 at the age of 15. In appearance he was short and slender, but strong. A chronicler describes him as 'beauteous and winsome'. Edgar made full use of his strength and beauty, abducting a nun at the age of 17 who bore him a daughter. Later he removed, *à la* Uriah, the husband of the lady who later became his second wife. Murder, lust and cruelty pervade the air of Edgar's young manhood. If he founded forty monasteries and did penance for seven years, it was not without cause.

Why Bath was chosen for this momentous coronation must remain an open question. The Anglo-Saxon kings appreciated this part of Wessex. There were palaces at Cheddar, where King Edmund was nearly killed hunting near the gorge; Pucklechurch, where the same monarch was later assassinated; Frome, where King Edred died in 955; and Calne, the scene of an event in 978 when 'all the chief councillors of the English people fell from an upper storey except that Abbot Dunstan remained standing on a beam'.

Bath, too, had a palace which seems to have been popular, King Edwig referring to 'the pleasant warm baths' in a charter. The fact that it was a border town between the two great Kingdoms of Mercia and Wessex was probably the deciding factor.

The Saxon king, Osric, founded Bath Abbey in 676. About 100 years later the establishment was enlarged by King Offa, whose mighty dyke marking the boundary between Mercia and Wales was already old when Edgar was crowned. From being the personal property of the Mercian Royal House, Bath remained in the direct possession of the Kings of England until 1088 when William Rufus sold it to the Bishop of Wells who transferred his see there.

The Plantagenets were occasional visitors. King John was here in 1216, Edward I in 1276 and twice in 1286, staying five days on the second occasion. Henry VII passed through in 1497 when pursuing Perkin Warbeck. Queen Elizabeth I visited Bath in 1574 and came again in 1591. On this second occasion she drove in and almost immediately drove out again because of the stench of the open sewer. The cure was worse than the disease.

Elizabeth was notoriously sensitive about smells. Anne of Denmark, wife of James I, had other troubles when she came to take the waters in 1616. 'As the Queen was bathing in the King's Bath,' wrote the Reverend Richard Warner, 'there arose from the bottom of the cistern, just by the side of Her Majesty, a flame of fire like a candle which had no sooner ascended to the top of the water than it spread itself upon the surface into a large circle of light.' Anne was so frightened that she insisted on bathing in the bath used by the hoi polloi. It was later named the Queen's Bath.

In the next reign, Queen Henrietta Maria had thoughts of coming to Bath, but decided instead to take the waters of Bourbon in her native France. Her decision was a wise one if Bath was even half as bad at the time as Wood says:

> The streets and public ways of the city were become like so many dunghills, slaughter-houses and pig-styes . . . people washed every kind of thing they had to make clean at the common conduits; and nothing was more common than small racks and mangers at almost every door for the baiting of horses. The baths were like so many bear-gardens . . . people of both sexes bathing by day and by night naked; and dogs, cats, and pigs, even human creatures, were hurl'd over the rails into the water.

The next royal visit, that of Charles I and the Prince of Wales in 1644, was a grimmer affair. They came to trounce the Roundheads with 9,000 troops at their back. The King went on to Wells to stay in Sir John Horner's house while his son dined with Sir Ralph Hopton at Witham. It was 20 years before Bath saw more of the Stuart family. When Charles II came with Catherine of Braganza in 1663 it was in the hope of finding the waters 'remedial in sterility'. The weather was so bad that it was 10 days before the Queen could enter the bath, 'sweating vastly'.

They sallied forth to Longleat, only to have a hair-raising journey on the rough Somerset roads. The Queen swore that she would never again venture out in such a mountainous country. The Duke of York accompanied the sovereigns to Bath. He spent his time 'abed with his duchess' and examining such natural curiosities as the snails from Silbury Hill which he sent for from John Aubrey. Pepys was not there to record the royal ablutions, but he took the waters some years later, apparently his first bath for nine years. His sense of hygiene was shocked. 'Methinks,' he wrote, 'it cannot be clean to go so many bodies in the same water.'

Grapevine in the Sky

How the owls know where the vole populations are greatest

AN OBSERVER SWEEPING THE SKY CONTINUALLY WITH HIGH-powered glasses from the top of Birmingham's unmemorable cathedral would see passing over, in the course of a year, almost every bird on the British list. If a learned society would care to crown the cupola with an observatory, equip it with a swivelling charpoy and arrange for my sustenance, I will undertake the arduous task of providing the evidence necessary to support this important theory. My train of thought was inspired by a question put to me by a friend on how short-eared owls congregate so expediously when a vole population explodes into a plague. Salisbury Plain was his case in point. Short-eared owls, he said, were not usually seen on the plain; but let there be a vole plague and miraculously they materialise—but from where? And how is the news communicated? Thus the observatory in Birmingham.

The larger birds—especially the predators—spend far more time than has so far been recognised cruising at high altitudes, accomplishing journeys over considerable ranges as the spirit moves them, quite outside migratory activities. I have watched sparrowhawks in hill country intensively. Reference works mention prospecting flights prior to hunting, but apart from that the impression is given of a bird whose life is passed skulking in ambush or hedge-hopping to take prey by surprise. It does both; but times without number I have seen a sparrowhawk which had previously seemed to be prospecting for prey soar up to a height at which binocular-aided identification was solely by virtue of continuous observation from an adjacent point of departure. The maximum altitude is between 2,000 and 3,000ft. The figures on the Ordnance map for spot-heights and contours in the vicinity give one a scale of reference. Take a pair of binoculars to a vantage point 2,000ft above sea level on a clear day; check on a map what lies within your range of vision. Imagine you could, with the ease of sparrowhawk or buzzard, soar in a circle of 10 miles diameter. The area under effective scrutiny would be considerable.

I have watched every species of diurnal raptor in Britain —with the paradoxical exception of the short-eared owl— perform high altitude flights. If keen-sighted eyes should, at the extremity of their range, detect two or three other raptors converging on a target beyond the horizon then it is likely that curiosity would dictate pursuit. On a smaller geographical scale, I have seen this happen many times. The newly afforested areas in the Cambrians were last year a paradise both for raptors and those observing them. The vole explosion had occurred, and trees were not sufficiently grown to obscure vistas. The area is vast and vole concentrations were patchy. The kestrels were the reconnaissance force. Let but two or three hang in the air for half an hour over a square kilometre of conifer seedlings and they would be joined by two, three, four, sometimes as many as eight buzzards. If this concentration of hovering hawks persisted for another hour, one's chances of seeing short-eared owls, even a kite or a hen harrier, were worth betting on. It is well known that vultures detect carrion by noting the behaviour of other scavengers, possibly of hunters too.

Such a reaction should not seem strange to human beings. During the food rationing of World War II and its aftermath, there were many stories of people joining queues outside shops purely because the existence of a queue implied there was something worth queueing for.

Short-eared owls are good enough naturalists to know that what is of interest to kestrels and buzzards concerns them, too. I have yet to see the bird soar up out of sight on a prospecting flight, but I live in expectation. All birds may practise methods of communication outside our present ken; science advances; there is far more to be learned than has so far been added to the store of human knowledge. In the field of bird communication, nothing would surprise me; but until new discoveries render it obsolete, I am for the theory of high flight coupled with keen sight as the raptors' techniques for assembling on prey concentrations—linked with a tendency to keep an eye on each other.

It is interesting to follow through from concentration to the collapse and dispersal stage of the cycle. When every tussock of cotton-grass conceals a vole-run, short-eared owls may lay as many as a dozen eggs (twice the normal clutch size) and hatch them all. Voles are in such plentiful supply that there is abundant food for all nestlings hatched. Hunting is so easy that one parent may remain permanently on guard against buzzard, harrier and prowling fox. Thus the owl population, together with that of all other vole-predators, rises rapidly. Then comes the vole crash; precipitated not by predation but by epidemic disease. Expanded populations of short-eared owls, of harriers, buzzards, kestrels—and foxes— find themselves on short commons. Next breeding season, the raptors automatically reduce clutch sizes.

The search for prey becomes highly competitive and an unceasing task for both parents, thus aggravating the situation so that nestlings are left unbrooded to die of exposure or unguarded to vanish into the maw of some other vole-deprived predator. Faster than it rose, the local raptor population collapses. One wonders what happens to the adult short-eared owls. The usual migratory habits of the species are likely to move them south and east in the autumn to take advantage of fresh hunting grounds, or at least those which have survived the herculean labour of hunting to feed hungry nestlings when the prey are operating a 'Sellers' Market'. Some will certainly have succumbed to the weakness and malnutrition attendant upon their inescapable instinctive duty. Nature is ruthless: but in all ways one detects a force working for balance and stability, for the survival of species, if not of the individual member.

Salute to the Rains

And a private rite of thanksgiving on drinking a glass of water

NOBODY CAN JUSTLY ACCUSE ME OF BEING A HEAVY DRINKER OF water. But from time to time I take a glass, and when this happens it is generally the occasion for a small private ceremony. Those who have learned the value of water the hard way will understand. I hold the glass up to the light and enjoy the knowledge that it is actually there, that it is clear and cold, and that it is all for me to drink, at one draught if I wish. I thank God for the major blessing of its presence in my hand, and for the minor ones of its translucence in contrast to some of the murky samples which have come my way, and of its freedom from the taste of chlorine.

As I swallow it, memories form a backcloth to what some may consider an uninspiring celebration. I think again of days when one army bottleful of brownish liquid, often containing small dead fish, hot by day, malodorous by night, and as nauseating as it was obsessive, had to last 48 hours and sometimes 72; days when the big decision was not whether one could afford to take more than one mouthful, but whether that mouthful could actually be swallowed or should be spat back into the bottle to be savoured again later, beastly though it was.

We who shared such interludes know as something more than mere theory that water is the Creator's lifeline to the human race. With water we could hope to live to eat the next meal, however long it might be delayed. With food, but no water, expectation of life could be calculated in hours.

It is no surprise to me that Moses made so deep an impression on his people when, in their hour of crisis, he smote upon the rock. I once saw a similar feat performed, with results equally far reaching for his 150 comrades, by a bombardier in Burma. With his axe, pick, general service, he smote upon the desiccated shale. The little hole he made filled within half an hour with a six-inch depth of water. Not much, but enough for men who, like Coleridge's seafarers, had gone a night and a day with 'throats unslaked and black lips baked'. When I asked why he had done what he did at that particular spot, he recalled something he had learned as

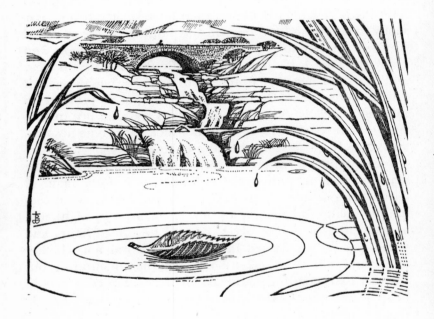

a Boy Scout and added that he had since become a water diviner. To us he seemed, and indeed was, the agent of Almighty providence. In a place where no sapling grew for many miles he could not exercise his art but had acted from forgotten knowledge, and a half-blind faith.

When the chance came later, I made sure he taught me divining. The term is well chosen. I found the feat within my power, and have since employed it usefully. That I, or anybody else, can find water through the uncontrollable twisting of living wood in passive hands no longer seems remarkable to me. No such gift is bestowed upon us for the discovery of anything else than water. But there is nothing else which we cannot, in the last accounting, do without.

When summer gives way to the equinoctial gales, and wet storms from the west I shall bear with limited patience people complaining that 'it' is raining. Let the rains come. And let us, for a change, be grateful for what we are about to receive, and which we waste so profligately. When the rains sweep across the countryside, drumming through starless nights, bouncing off the gutters, splashing into water butts, flowing milkily in runnels from the chalk, or chocolate brown from blocked field drains in loam and clay, raising river-voices from trickles, to gurgles, to roaring floods, we hear and see the Almighty's elemental gift to all life here below. I for one lift up my heart.

The Deerhound

When you and I are past and dead
  Will any then remember
That we walked the hill in the dawning red,
  And smile, that we loved December?

A wet grey wind is on the hill,
  Only the two of us here.
I muse and dream as a human will;
  You race with a phantom deer.

Son of the wind, with your strength and speed,
  A bare twelve months you own,
But yours is the splendour of Fingal's breed
  Who hunted the deer alone.

GAVIN A. MACLAREN

The Welsh and English Wye

The split personality of a great river, with hwyl upstream and serenity down

RIVERS ARE LIKE ANIMALS, PARTICULARLY HUMAN ONES. THEY are greatly influenced by climate and topography. Like the mountain stream, the mountain man is quick and volatile; like the rivers of flat country, the plain dweller is slow and stable in temperament. But unlike most humans, rivers often have a split personality. They are slow, sometimes placid, as they near the sea, but wild and turbulent in the head waters. No river epitomises this dichotomy more than the Wye; the bottom half is as English as cricket, the upper is as Welsh as an eisteddfod.

The Hay area is the dividing point, and since this is border country (there are plenty of places prefixed Pen- or Pont- on the English side) a mutual suspicion still exists. Although there is more than a hint of Welsh in the Herefordshire voice, to be described as 'welshy' is anything but a compliment.

The two halves of the river are like the two national characters, although from a practical point of view they are both deceptive. The English half is broad, relatively open, smooth but concealing hidden depths. The Welsh half is quick moving, ebullient but more predictable than would appear. The bed of the Wye is often treacherous and wading is sometimes difficult and dangerous.

Moseivitch was once asked why one of the other great pianists of his time always looked so sad when playing at a concert. 'Maybe he does not like music', he replied. I feel like this on much of the English end of the Wye. If one is an angler, to fish is to be happy. Yet I never feel as happy as I should, except on one or two beats I know well, for the lower Wye is difficult to read. One is faced with long pools, often half a mile long with hardly a feature, which look readable but often are not. The first time I fished Winforton, I came to The Wall and thought: 'Now here is a bit of water I can work out.' I was about to wade in when the bailiff came down the other bank. 'I'd start in about 10 yards higher up,' he said. 'They usually lies just above that break.' On the first cast I had a fish and, although I had another where I expected one, local knowledge had doubled my catch.

Fly fishing on the English half can be difficult, for so often one is fishing a strong, solid glide and those popples of broken water, where the line is gripped and guided by the grain of the current, are few and far between. This end is littered by those who live some way from its banks, Midlanders who fish for salmon on a day-a-week basis.

As one moves upstream into Wales, the whole scene changes, and as far as I am concerned (this is not chauvinism) changes for the better. The river becomes smaller and faster and I fish without the feeling of being overwhelmed by its size and shapelessness. One can go to strange water, look at it and say to oneself, 'Fish should lie between there and there'—and they do.

There is also a sense of intimacy which is not only to do with the smaller size of water. Here the river is part of local life. You share the water with the local postman with a rod tied to the crossbar of his bicycle rather than an industrialist arriving in an expensive car. There is a general interest in fishing, particularly in salmon fishing. News of a big catch rapidly becomes common knowledge up the river. Here the countryside is as wild and exciting as the river and its salmon. This is the country of the polecat and the buzzard. Not far away there are red kites and other less rare hawks if one knows where to look. Yet although it is wild country, it is rarely stark. In spring and summer, when softened by flowers, it is as colourful as the Welsh adjectives in the place-names.

The Wye is a river of great and varying beauty. Rising in

the bogs of Plynlimmon, it flows as a rocky stream containing small, beautifully coloured trout until it reaches Llangurig. There it changes to a salmon river. Some fish reach these upper waters early in the season and the small pools by the back end are often filled with fish that are harried by methods both legal and illegal. The lower end of the Wye could be left open twelve months in the year and no damage would be done, but these salmon, which have battled their way through the ocean and up to the headwaters, deserve sanctuary from prawn, treble and gaff. A fish which has swum so far should be left to spawn in peace.

From Llangurig down to Rhayader the river flows swiftly over rock to divide Radnorshire from Brecknockshire. It is joined by the Elan in whose valley the City Fathers of Birmingham built their reservoirs. Soon it is joined on the left bank by the Ithon and on the right by the Irfon at Builth. Salmon and trout run both rivers, although the river system now supports a strong population of coarse fish.

Many would claim the cream of the Wye lies between Builth and Hay. If it is not the best, it is for me the best-looking and the most interesting. From Hay, the river flows fast but less broken through softening countryside to the city of Hereford, through apple orchards to delight the eye in spring and through high-hedge hopfields to Ross. Between the two towns the river flows in wide loops and at Mordiford is joined by the Lugg, much cursed by salmon fishermen, for when it runs red in spate it puts the Wye out of order below Luggmouth. However, its grayling offers more than compensation for me, and to watch the salmon scale Bodenham weir back-end is a sight to admire. The river loops, past hillsides of wild cherry, past the superb scenery of Symonds Yat, down to Monmouth, where, as Shakespeare said, 'there is salmons . . .' Here it is joined by the Monnow, as fair a trout stream as ever man cast fly on. And so to Chepstow and the Severn Sea; it flows straight at first, makes a loop at Tintern, a bigger one above Chepstow, before merging first with the Severn and then the Usk.

76

Hunting the Human

A farmer's wife gave the bloodhounds a 13-mile run before they caught her

MORE THAN THREE CENTURIES AGO, A HOUND VERY MUCH LIKE the bloodhound was being used for hunting man. It was, perhaps, a little shorter on the leg and not always black and tan in marking. This hound was, in fact, the St Hubert, named after the patron saint of hunting himself and originally brought over from France by Norman knights. Since that time, a particular strain of the St Hubert had been bred for the purpose of tracking down poachers of deer and stealers of cattle, and from this has descended the bloodhound of today.

A bloodhound's greatest asset is its nose. I have watched one follow the scent of a man who had a line twelve hours earlier. This was on 'clean boot', that is with no artificial drag. The hound is acquainted with the scent of its quarry by means of a 'clue', something which the quarry has worn or handled. If it is intended that a bloodhound shall do the work for which it was bred, hunting man, then it must never be allowed to stoop to any other scent; anything else should be regarded as riot. Nor should any artificial aid such as aniseed ever be used.

Before World War II, there had been one or two packs of bloodhound hunting the carted deer, the best known being the Ranston. In the 'thirties, I whipped-in to five couple hunting clean boot. But this practice of hunting them as a pack was frowned upon by many breeders, who declared the bloodhound was essentially an individual that should not be expected to go to cry. Each hound should be allowed to work out the line of the quarry to its own satisfaction.

At the end of World War II, very few, if any, bloodhounds

77

were left in Britain and a number were imported from the USA. Among those who set out to revive the breed was Mr Eric Furness, of Brampton Old Hall, Chesterfield. He was of the opinion that possibly through unavoidable inbreeding the bloodhound lacked stamina. No hound should be exhausted after hunting a four-mile line. There was another weakness, a proneness to a malady aptly termed abdominal distension. When afflicted with this, the hound 'blew up' in the manner of some unfortunate sheep and, although temporary relief could be given, death nearly always resulted. I have seen this distension in only one other canine and that was an otterhound.

Mr Furness hunted the Peak Bloodhounds as a pack on clean boot and gave them up only a year or two ago on his doctor's advice. To improve stamina and eliminate distension, he introduced an out-cross in his kennel by using Dumfriesshire foxhound blood. In defending himself against purist critics, he states that the greatest bloodhound breeder of all time, the late Edwin Brough, recommended an outcross every five years. The result of this particular foxhound cross is a very workmanlike stamp of hound with less 'lumber' and wrinkle than the pure-bred bloodhound. I have heard breeders of the past maintaining that 'wrinkle', the folds of skin on the face, indicate a 'cold nose', the ability to pick up a scent long after it has been left, but this has never been proved to my satisfaction.

Hunting the clean boot has one advantage over the pursuit of a wild quarry in that the line taken by the runner can be arranged beforehand. This means that in a country like that hunted by the Peak, hunting could go on after foxhunting had ceased. On some days, spring hunting brought out mounted fields of eighty to ninety and, on one occasion, the field included nine MFHs. I asked about the endurance of hounds and was told that it was customary to hunt three lines in the course of a day, each of at least four miles in length. One hour's 'law' was allowed to the runner before the pack was laid on. The young wife of a farmer appears to have been one of the best runners and it is on record that on one day in particular she ran 13 miles in front of hounds.

This out-cross to Dumfriesshire foxhound, a strain with bloodhound in its breeding, has certainly not meant any loss in nose. Mr Furness told me that his hounds have owned a line through three inches of snow. When I saw them, they appeared to have terrific drive, far more than that of the pure-bred. Also, they went to cry, probably because they had always been hunted as a pack.

When the Peak Bloodhounds were given up, the hounds went to other packs, of which there are now four in England, all hunting clean boot and being hunted from the saddle. Most if not all of these hounds can be traced back to the Peak and so have Dumfriesshire foxhound in their veins. The latest pack is the Windsor Forest Bloodhounds, formed by officers of The Blues and Royals in 1971 to hunt a country loaned by the Garth and South Berks Foxhounds.

Winter Sunset

> *In the woods leaves lie shed,*
> *Which yesterday in gold and red*
> *Shone along the hill;*
> *While they now show dark and dead*
> *The colours from the woodlands fled*
> *Suffuse the sunset still;*
> *A sign that from this silent ground*
> *Spring will rise with blossom crowned,*
> *And woods with singing thrill.*
>
> G. H. JENNINGS

Mice and Men

More in sorrow than in anger, an admission of the impossibility of co-existence

NIP IN THE AIR AT NIGHT HAS SENT THE MICE INDOORS. Outposts of our house show evidence of infiltration. Now is the time to frustrate their knavish tricks, if necessary by slaying the little devils. The prospect brings no pleasure. To regard as enemies beneath one's roof such visitors as are unquestionably present in force beneath mine is uncomfortable for one whose relations with wildlife continue to be friendly. To trap seekers for shelter is the negation of hospitality, even if the necessity be undeniable.

By their tawny fronts and grey stomachs I deduce that ours are field mice, not house mice. Their readiness to move outdoors again in spring confirms this. They have clean glossy beauty. They also have the characteristics of mice the world over. The first is that although they have much to gain by keeping quiet they are quite incredibly noisy. One would not believe creatures so small capable of being heavy-footed. But they are. Here in my dressing room, at the end of the corridor far from the madding crowd, silence generally reigns. Not now. Using some secret track inside the walls, probably as old as any right of way in the village, mice have reoccupied the void above the ceiling. There they will stay through the hard weather months. And there, now, they are keeping themselves sound in wind and limb. Apparently they play some mouse-version of Rugby football. The rumble of their hoofbeats overhead as they form rucks and breakaways resembles a stampede of bison in a Wild West film. The sheer cheek and confidence of their behaviour amazes me. One would expect creatures reputedly furtive to conceal rather than advertise exercise of squatter's rights.

They have, of course, weighed me up accurately. Slow to wrath (and somewhat idle), I shall take no action unless they commit a hostile act. This they have never done in eight winters as my neighbours. One came near it when I saw him shinning up the canvas case of a trout rod. But he seemed to know where he was going, and I wished him well. Had any lady of the household been present, a breach of the peace would have occurred. Another characteristic of mice is the hostility they evoke from womenkind.

The distaff side, except when juvenile, have no sympathy for the wee cowerin' sleekit timorous beasties of Robert Burns. They see only the incarnation of all that is unnerving and evil. Even to suspect a mouse is for them to demand counter-measures. Already this autumn one mouse has attracted adverse publicity. My wife found it when she went to bed. It was couched on her electric blanket and was, moreover, reluctant to leave. Small blame to it on a chilly night. My suggestion that there was room for both of them received a dusty answer. Its appearance extended the zone of potential hostilities.

This permanently includes the apartment known, grandiloquently, as the boot hall. There footwear is changed, pony feeds prepared, and the door left open. To hear some recent situation reports, one might think mice had been marching in by column of threes. Outraged looks accompany these announcements and awaken that irrational sense of personal responsibility which is the burden all husbands bear. So, since a man's first duty is to defend his family against the malevolence of the brute creation, out come the traps. The annual battle of wits, humiliating if I lose and disagreeable if I win, begins again. My plans are second nature now.

Another characteristic of mice is that, clan by clan and generation after generation, they always do the same thing. The boot hall mice are heading for a warm corner near the boiler room. There they may eat stored tulip bulbs, search the pockets of my oldest shooting jacket for bits of dog biscuit, and drink condensation off an outflow pipe. Not for long. One by one the traps will catch them. The season's bag will be about thirty. It always is. I am not amused. My wish is that all the mice would be my guests and live in peace in that void above the ceiling over my head as I write. Mice have never done harm there, and the addition of another 120 pounding feet could not greatly alter the already stupendous bedlam which the present occupants are creating.

The Land-Rover's Jubilee

In praise of a vehicle which has changed the life of Britons where the pavements end

THE LAND-ROVER'S FIRST QUARTER-CENTURY CAME IN 1973. IN 25 years this solid motor has won a place in the scenery not only of Britain, but of the whole world's rugged places. No vehicle has excelled it in continued usefulness, and few have equalled it. In Britain it has achieved more than respect. It has a charisma astonishing for a mere artefact of transportation. It has woven itself into rural life, and especially into the pleasanter parts of it.

In fields and forestry, and on engineering sites, it is the go-anywhere-and-do-anything partner of hard-working men. To farm bailiffs and gamekeepers a personal 'Rover' ('Land' has long dropped from common parlance) is both prerequisite and status symbol. It has replaced the farmer's cob, the covert-hack, and the genuine shooting brake. It has carried guns, then ladies and dogs—all tossed together in traditional intimacy as it rolls over the tractor ruts—on millions of shooting days. It has towed horse trailers to and from meets, shows, gymkhanas, and point-to-points.

There never was, and probably never will be, anything like it. Square, tough and practical, it was never meant to be beautiful and certainly is not comfortable nor, like most hard workers, is a Land-Rover always clean. Yet no eyebrow is raised when dinner guests drive up in one, and emerge immaculate. The BBC long ago gave up their coy practice of calling it 'a field car' lest its maker's name leaked out. The whole globe knows it as something both special and unique. Its designers have never sought to change its basic structure, though they have constantly improved it.

To the ex-soldiers of World War II, to whom any attempt

to rival, let alone excel, its American forerunner the jeep seemed an impertinence doomed to failure, it began as an upstart. It is now a pillar of society in the countryside. No other everyday appurtenance has made more things easier, and some possible, or been regarded with so near-personalised affection. Here is some of its history.

Land-Rovers have become such an accepted part of life in so many different countries of the world, that it is difficult to see how we could ever have managed without them. The legend of the Land-Rover began in 1948 at the Solihull factory of the Rover company and, over its quarter century, it has created for itself a unique personality amongst automobiles. It is far more than just another vehicle and has been a leading character in stories of adventure and achievement throughout the world. Early in 1947, several short, sturdy, working-type vehicles were seen running around on agricultural land near Rover's Solihull works. They were doing various jobs—one was towing a trailer loaded with milk churns, another pulling hay-raking equipment, another dragging an 8ft tandem-disc harrow and yet another generating a circular saw. On other days they would be performing another series of agricultural tasks. These activities went on at Solihull for a number of months and whilst a certain air of secrecy prevailed at the works, it became known that the vehicles were actually prototypes of a new 'go-anywhere' type of vehicle that would carry the name 'Land-Rover'.

It was at the Amsterdam Motor Show in 1948 that the Land-Rover was first announced. Rover's new four-wheel drive, off-road vehicle was soon shown to the British public and was acclaimed a winner. Quantity production of the Land-Rover commenced in July 1948 and has continued without a break to today's weekly output of some 1,200 vehicles.

During its highly successful career, the Land-Rover has changed very little in outward appearance, but the Rover engineers proudly proclaim that they have redesigned and improved every component. As is the way with all but the

84

most expensive motor cars, the Land-Rover is manufactured on a production-line basis. Each vehicle is, however, basically handmade. The aluminium bodywork is made up from a number of panels, each welded electronically in sub-assemblies. Then each assembly is treated for rust prevention and paint sprayed. Finally, the vehicle is built up on the immensely strong chassis and suspension on a low-moving conveyor. Its makers claim that the Land-Rover is 'the world's most versatile vehicle', and surely nobody could dispute that. It is this very versatility that has made the Land-Rover so acceptable to agricultural and construction people, not only in the UK, but in most countries around the world.

Each Land-Rover is virtually tailor-made for its prospective owner. The choice of engines, body styles, power take-offs and accessories is so enormous that Land-Rovers find themselves doing the most amazing variety of tasks. The Land-Rover is equally at home on the ploughed fields of a Wiltshire farm and the searing heat of a Sahara track. Used extensively by the world's armies, the vehicle finds access to the most inaccessible spots—there is even a lightweight military version that can be carried by helicopter. It is sometimes the only means of transport for explorers or medical teams in the under-developed countries. Indeed, the Land-Rover is probably as familiar a sight on the African continent as it is here. One can see virtually no limit to the Land-Rover's abilities which have been so thoroughly proved over its illustrious 25 years. Probably this most popular of vehicles will become obsolete one day, but it will have to be a remarkable vehicle indeed that puts the Land-Rover into its grave. No doubt we shall see it reach its fiftieth birthday—and it will probably look just the same.

And Still the Austin Seven

How more than 500 went on a ceremonial drive to celebrate 50 years on the road

EVERYONE HAS BIRTHDAYS, BUT FEW WILL ADMIT HOW MANY. For the Austin Seven, however, 1972 was a proud year, marking the golden jubilee of the model's birth. The Austin Seven was the brainchild of Lord Austin (then Sir Herbert). It was designed by him, so rumour has it, on his billiard table. He intended it for the man who aspired to own a car, but could only afford a motor-cycle and sidecar. Like so many success stories, the beginning was hazardous. So depressed was the Austin Motor Company after the first war that it was with the greatest difficulty that Sir Herbert persuaded his board of directors to proceed with the car. So the Baby Austin was born beneath clouds in 1922.

It was called the Austin Seven Tourer but became nicknamed the 'Chummy', partly because it was less than four feet wide, also because its little hood embraced all four seats instead of leaving the back passengers out in the cold in a 'dickey', as was then the fashion. It cost £225. Success was not immediate. However, as it gained popularity the price was reduced. The Austin Motor Company had been saved. The range increased with the introduction of the fabric saloon in 1926, followed by a metal saloon and sporting versions. Fifty-one different body styles were produced, most of them by private coach builders, and by the time production of the Ruby and Big Seven saloons was halted by hostilities in 1939, well over a quarter of a million Austin Sevens had been made.

The secret of its success is hard to define. Perhaps it was sweet simplicity, for although its road-holding and braking left much to be desired, you could always depend on the

Austin Seven. Like so many legends, there was more to the Austin Seven than a small family car. Despite its engine size of only three-quarters of a litre, it had a big heart that found its way into the most unusual places. The stories are endless, but an Austin Seven has climbed Ben Nevis (and returned the same day) while another performed on the stage of a pre-war musical hall.

Sevens have been round the world more times than they care to remember. Neither are these achievements confined to the history books. The most recent voyage was completed only last year. And what better way to celebrate a fiftieth anniversary than a run from Land's End to John O'Groats? Nearly 70 took part, and the quickest car completed the journey in 21 hours.

Then there were the supercharged racing Sevens pioneered by Gordon England, which did such battle with the MGs despite the limitations of a side-valve engine. Sir Herbert was quick to recognise the publicity to be gained from racing, but did he envisage so many world speed records when he originally designed that two-bearing crankshaft? Several class records still stand, although it would be foolish to pretend that modern machinery would be incapable of breaking them if it tried. Perhaps it is a matter of courtesy that few people have. Only in the latter years of Austin Seven production did the racing Sevens depart radically from their bread-and-butter relations. The Murray Jamieson cars of 1936–9 had supercharged engines with twin overhead camshafts which, although of only 744cc capacity, produced a staggering 116 brake horsepower on sprint fuel. (It is said that their valve life under these conditions was seven minutes.) The intended 12,000rpm was never realised, since the war halted further development, but not before the winged motif had lapped Brooklands at an all-time class record of 121·2mph.

To mark the occasion of the golden jubilee, a commemorative rally was organised. For the Austin Seven it was a pilgrimage, the factory at Longbridge witnessing over 500 of the little cars. This provided me with the unexpected opportunity of a drive in an Austin Ulster sports car; to savour briefly the bygone motoring joys of the thirties. Austin Ulsters are now rare. This one had been perfectly restored by its owner, Mr Reg Nice. It was made in 1930 and is now valued conservatively at over £1,000.

Bright red, the Ulster has a charming appearance, with its stubby bonnet, cheeky pointed tail, no doors and a large fishtail exhaust not far from the passenger's left ear. Climbing over the side, I found the cockpit so narrow that my right arm had to travel outside the bodywork. The starter motor protrudes into the car from the engine compartment. Its engagement sounds violent. The engine splatters to life, and is unexpectedly responsive to the throttle. It is all great fun. There are only three ratios at the end of the long floppy gearstick. The clutch has only about one inch to travel, and its sensitivity is helped by the fact that you can feel the rubbing of the plates through the sole of your shoe. The whine of the gears is truly vintage, with a splendid rasp from the exhaust on the overrun. Second gear can achieve 50mph, while the top speed is in the region of 68mph. Not a bad performance for a standard Seven sports engine of 1930. The cable brakes were heavy and rudimentary, pulling slightly to the right. I did not notice any weather protection.

Quite why the Austin Seven should evoke such enthusiasm compared with other small cars of its day is hard to say. Is it necessary to ask? During the cavalcade that followed the rally, the sight and sound of several hundred of those tall, narrow little saloons hooting to each other with excitement as they threaded the streets of Birmingham, was a moving experience indeed.

Our Cottage Gardens

*How the countryman tamed the wild flowers, and why it all
began with the Black Death*

AMONG THE MOST VIVID MEMORIES OF MY CHILDHOOD DAYS ARE
the smells encountered on school holidays spent in the country. Perhaps the finest is the delicious fragrance of the
massed flowers in cottage gardens. Historically, the cottage
garden seems to have appeared at the beginning of the fif-
teenth century and soon became a feature of the English
countryside. This was after the Black Death of 1349, when
the mortality among farmworkers placed a premium on their
labour. In some cases, the more enterprising were able to
rent stretches of land, which had become fallow through
shortage of labour, and in effect became tenant farmers. The
rest obtained substantially greater rewards from their labour.

Becoming richer, the workers built themselves cottages,
often with gardens. In them, they grew herbs for flavouring,
potions and lotions which had been confined to the monasteries, and vegetables to feed their families. Initially, there
was no place for flowers, but gradually the farmhand trans-
lated to his garden something that attracted him in the
hedgerows. Flower seeds, carried by the wind or wandering
animals, were left undisturbed to germinate or a plant given
by a friendly neighbour was set. As time passed, flowers in
their masses sprang up among the vegetables and herbs.
Thus, the cottage garden was created.

Whatever might be the source of its occupants, the rule in
the cottage garden was unruliness. There grew cabbages,
catmint, marjoram, marigolds, daffodils, daphne, lilies, loosestrife, fuchias, fennel, irises, candytuft, tansy, tagetes, hya-
cinth, horseradish, paeonies, potentillas, bourbon roses and
sweet briar hedges all woven together with honeysuckle and

hosts of other plants scenting the air from morn to night. It was untold beauty created at no cost. The hedgerows, friends, natives, the lord of the manor, neighbouring yeomen and other country people were the benefactors. No time was spent on cultivation, everything grew naturally, relying on rain for watering and the fallen debris for plant food. The close planting did the mulching by creating shade at the roots. Occasion-

ally there was a load of muck from the pigsty or the chicken run. There were no lawns and edges to cut or paths to weed because any seedlings that grew in the cracks added still greater beauty to the ensemble.

A small garden might be a peaceful retreat from the pressures of the rat-race, where the demands on time, labour and money do not impinge themselves. It might appear revolutionary to turn a small garden entirely into a cottage garden, but it is an idea that might attract much envy and create imitations among the neighbours.

In creating a cottage garden, there are few stipulations. However, care must be taken to see that the strongest plants do not overwhelm the weaker. Heights, colours, perfumes and architectural forms are mixed indiscriminately, for disorder is the secret of success. Often care is no onerous task; no hoeing or weeding, perhaps merely an annual dressing of garden compost. The plants propagate themselves by broadcasting their own seeds, while others throw out runners and suckers. Nothing need be lifted and divided until the quality of their flowers diminish. In some cases, this might mean every 10 years.

To start a cottage garden, a collection of plants is needed. To those already mentioned above might be added hypericums, genista, witchhazel, lilac, mock orange, lavender, rosemary, ivy, box, arabis, black-eyed susans, canterbury bells, violets, dahlias, daisies, day lilies, evening primroses, golden rod, herb robert, jasmine, larkspur, London pride, lupins, Michaelmas daisies, monkshood, pinks, poppies, polyanthus, moonflowers, scarlet pimpernel, giant sunflowers, sweet peas, tobacco plants, wallflowers and antirrhinums.

If more and more gardeners create a cottage garden patch, in which many will seed themselves, numbers of these lovely flowers of the past will be preserved, even after they have vanished from the seedsmen's catalogues. Not only are they beautiful, but historically they have also given pleasure to countryfolk for many years. Among those that most readily come to mind is the charming sweetly-scented little plant, Mignonette, which older readers particularly will recall as a childhood joy. There is the biennial, *Lunaria biennis*, mysteriously popularly called Honesty, which was probably known to Chaucer. Its great beauty lies in its intriguing, flat, satiny-white seed pods, like moons, the size of a 10p piece, which were produced when dried and graced every Edwardian parlour throughout the winter.

Another lovely annual, which is seen infrequently nowadays and could easily disappear altogether, is Scarlet Pimpernel, *Anagallis arvensis,* a native wildflower that was adopted by the cottagers long ago. Its charms were sung by the early nineteenth-century poet, John Clare, in *Shepherds' Calendar for May.* In addition to its loveliness, it served as an old-time forecast of rain; its flowers failed to open when this was likely.

There are many other beautiful subjects of the past whose existence is threatened by modern living; love-lies-bleeding, hollyhock, London pride, cowslips, the half-hardy climber, *Thunbergia alata* (black-eyed susan), *Ranunculus aconiti-folius* ('fair maids of France') and cherry pie. It would indeed be a great tragedy if these and others like them vanished.

The Attic

Through the blurred window sunlight stabs and spills
In golden pools upon the attic floor,
To stir the past, evoking tender ghosts
That lie in trance-like sleep behind the door.
The rocking horse, hemmed in by musty books
Still stares with arrogant and fiery eyes,
While drunkenly, the battered doll's house leans
Against a case of captive butterflies.
Familiar faces peer from cobwebbed frames,
A school trunk props a broken easy chair,
And on a pile of shrimping nets and pails
Forlornly sits a faded teddy-bear.
Each cherished object in this dusty room,
The sunlight's benediction will receive,
For all the joy and happiness it gave
To children's magic world of make-believe.

KAY WORNE

A Swift in the Hand

On the riverside, a strange encounter; its sequel, a new understanding

AGAIN, THE SWIFTS HAVE GONE. REALISATION OF THEIR absence is an annual landmark. The cuckoo merely fades away; his song ceased weeks ago. When the swifts depart one can almost feel the silence. On summer evenings they fly in packs, winging down the village street, screaming 'swee-swee' as if in exultation at their speed, while at one-fifth of their velocity the village youths do likewise on drop-handlebar bicycles and signalise their prowess by much ringing of bells. Birds above and boys below give a sound-pattern of joy in living, and now half of it is missing. And yet, in a very minor way, that silence brings me peace of mind. Henceforth I can fish for trout with one worry fewer. A swift once took my fly, and I would not wish it to happen again. There is no way of preventing it. Until they have migrated the hazard exists.

It was late afternoon on a chalk stream. The sun's angle was now sideways to the stream, not upon it from above. This dictated a change in tactics for me; also, it seemed, for the swifts. Down they came from those strata in the middle air where, unseen by us, they hunt by day and are reputed often to sleep through the short summer nights. There was a harvest of flies over the water. In line astern, they flashed upstream as fast as cricket balls from a fast bowler, low to the surface, swerving and banking. Then they swung out over the meadows in a half-mile arc to join the river far below and come speeding up it again. They cut the air as they went by, as if sails were spilling all wind.

Why, I wondered, do they not hunt the water downstream? At least a fly-fisherman would then see them coming. But always it is upstream, or so it seems to me. And always, therefore, the back cast goes out to meet them as they come. Mentally, I was prepared for the impact when one took. At 100mph the most discerning swift could hardly be blamed for failure to distinguish between my Lunn's Particular and whatever he sought. So I was ready to stop the forward cast and let the line drop behind me.

Turning, wading down, reeling in, the line led to a clump of loosestrife on the bank. The swift lay, unhurt, unresisting, and unfrightened, in the grass beyond it. For the first time I held in my hand, and studied in stillness, what I had hitherto known only as a thing of headlong speed. It felt light, soft, warm; incredible that this delicate and gentle creature could lance the air with such contemptuous power. It looked black with small whitish tufts, not the dull black of a bat, but a brilliant black which glossed green and bronze. Its eye was soft, dark and calm; its bill almost non-existent, more like a mouth with horny lips. In a corner was my fly. It came easily away.

Relieved, I looked at the swift. Relieved, the swift looked at me. And so the strange encounter. I had seen thousands of swifts as dark scimitars wheeling at great height or flashing past me. Swifts must look down on men in millions, slow, earthbound, inexplicable. For once the twain had met. The dark eyes turned this way and that, taking in the surroundings with calm interest. Apart from its nesting ledge, had it ever known before so much immobility in daylight? Trees, reeds, me, all to be studied and checked upon instead of left behind, must have opened up to it a new world of arrested motion.

Feeling similarly, but in reverse, I pondered how to entertain, and how release, my guest. Perhaps it had suffered shock, and was unfit to fly until it had rested. Certainly it showed no disposition to do so. I opened my hand. The swift lay there in evident comfort. So I carried it back to the fishing hut, a building well-stricken with years and huddled now in old age amid rosebay and young alders. I put the swift on the roughened, sloping roof. And there it lay, clinging with feet that were prehensile but of little use for walking. Swifts, having no use for so mundane a form of locomotion, probably do not walk 20 yards in the whole of their lives.

While I drank a cup of tea the swift surveyed its limited scene with polite resignation. Other swifts were dashing past. It shifted its grip as it watched them go, but made no attempt to fly. The truth dawned on me slowly, being unscientifically orientated. So efficient a flyer, so inefficient a walker, could not attain take-off speed without height to dive. The fishing hut was too low. So I took him in my hand again. A creature without foes, he settled there contentedly. I waded into the stream, telling him as we went to watch out next time and, if he saw a fisherman, to choose another bit of river. Then, our brief encounter nearing its end, we awaited the next flight of swifts.

When it came, I threw him high in the air. Momentarily, I thought he would stall and fall in the river. But, master of his element, he delayed levelling out until he had picked up flying speed. Then he was gone. I did not fish again that evening, but sat and watched the swifts.

A Lapidomaniac's Tale

To polish pebbles becomes a cult for a beachcomber with a creative eye

THE HOBBY OF STONE AND PEBBLE POLISHING HAS BECOME popular. Indeed, ever since I purchased a machine, the cult has taken a hold of our family and, like many other households, our way of life has changed. Now wherever we go, we are always searching for suitable ammunition for our treasured gadget. As we scan a beach here, a neighbour's drive there, we are intent on adding to our collection of gleaming baubles which are the product of our endeavours. But as our stock increases we also become wiser.

Ours is a large machine because we like to polish large stones. Since it is necessary to have a good supply of small pebbles to mix with them we achieve a double result, a quantity of large polished stones and a multitude of tiny polished pebbles suitable for making into jewellery. If our failures are disheartening, lessons are soon learned. Now we scrutinise what we collect with greater thoroughness, discarding those specimens which are of the wrong material or have flaws or cracks in them however beautiful they may be. Only when they are wet is it possible to foresee their appearance when polished.

Our tumbler cost over £20, but there are smaller models from £5 upwards. The three sizes of grit we use—80, 200 and 600 (our finest)—the cerium or tin oxide and pieces of chamois leather, polystyrene or wooden pellets necessary for the polishing are not so expensive. To polish 5lb weight of stones costs approximately £1. It is advisable to keep a tumbler out of earshot, though it must be near an electric point and have water available to wash the drum and its contents before the next grade of grit is used. Once the grit process and the few days of polishing have been completed, the stones must be cleansed in the drum with detergent, which must not be of the intensified or dish-washing variety.

The pleasures of the enterprise lie not so much in the tumbling and the polishing but in the finding of suitable material. Stone-gathering can be hard on the back and unless there are delectable samples on the shore it is easier to sit and sift, searching for rounded pebbles. However, the sea is not the only store of stones. A gravel drive will suffice.

The pastime can result in abortive journeys. Porlock, much lauded as a haven for stone-collectors, involved a 100 mile journey by car in each direction, a long and arduous walk across stony and muddy terrain. We returned with bags, baskets and pails full of enticing green and grey, smooth rocks. On introduction to the tumbler they proved to be impervious to the coarsest grit and worthless. In a tiny bay in Sutherland, it was necessary to brave enormous breakers to gather a harvest which appeared second to none as it lay in the chamber-pot. But all these stones were full of flaws, polished indifferently or broke up and were not worth the danger and soaking their collection entailed.

At Smoo caves, beloved of Sir Walter Scott, there were stones of perfect shape. Beautiful mottled black markings were abundant. We bent double to collect them and, afterwards, in full knapsacks carried them up the tortuous, steep path to the road, worn out but triumphant. A month later, we found that our haul was of no consequence. The stones would not polish. Nevertheless, the shores of Banffshire have provided us with some splendid, translucent and egg-like stones. Chesil Beach with acres of pebbles has also proved productive. Among such a wealth of material the collector can be selective, spurning the awkward shapes for the symmetrical and the attractive, for jewellery and for paper-weights.

The Senior Terrier

In the evening of her days, a silent communion with the other half of the partnership

EXCEPT FOR THE CHILDREN ASLEEP UPSTAIRS, I WAS ALONE IN the house that evening. My wife was attending that *sine qua non* of village life, a performance of *Blithe Spirit* in the Reading Room. Darkness had fallen and nobody else remained. I drank a little whisky and considered the next move. Would it be preferable to regale myself with Beethoven or Mozart? Or neither, but to listen instead to the wilder music of the wind as it eddied in the chimney and set the television aerial thrumming? In the event the record-player stayed silent. A new and mesmeric presence intervened.

Sitting on the arm of my chair, I realised, was the senior terrier. Her eyes were directed towards my face. It is three years since she saw me. Rising ten, she became suddenly and finally blind; and, being a fox terrier with all her lineage of courage and self-sufficiency, carried on much as usual. After nearly 13 years together we have small need nowadays of formal communication. We meet briefly at 7am when, after ceremonial yawning and stretching of stiffening limbs, she takes her first airing before Reveille sounds for the younger and more hobbledehoy gundogs. We seldom meet again until, all others having retired to bed or bath, I sit with a nightcap and think the thoughts that come with the ending of the day.

The senior terrier sits on the arm of the chair to think them with me. Tonight she was paying an unscheduled visit. She well knew that the evening was young because the junior terrier, not yet harboured in the kitchen, still slept post-prandially on the rug. Broken routine made the occasion

special. Ears cocked, she held the salute with her sightless
eyes. I returned her gaze, then stroked her neck. That she
did not move represented an eloquent speech. She is a fas-
tidious person and, though friendly to authorised strangers,
disdains their touch. Neither will she encourage mine if
there is an eye-witness to the familiarity. By remaining, she
made this a telepathic moment. So we shared thoughts
soundlessly, as one can with very old friends.

Her face, once bright tan with a blaze, is whitened now.
The grey slash from eye to muzzle, left by a fox in her active-
service days, has become invisible, merging with the sign of
advancing years, just as the incident itself has been cut down
to size by the other happenings of a long, full life. Old lady,
I thought, you are nearer the end than the beginning. And
realisation came late that the same applied to me.

Inevitably my mind turned to the business of growing old
gracefully, untroubling to others. When the time comes, I

hope I manage it as well as she does. In particular, I hope I shall be as meticulous as she is at keeping friendships green, and at evolving a design for living to fit declining powers.

She does not take much exercise nowadays. She even gave up the summer evening's stroll along the chalk track between the barley fields when asked to share it with a spaniel who, though well-meaning, had loutish manners. But she has no prejudice against youth in general. She chaperons the junior terrier with dignity, and is treated in response with the respect both given and taken by members of their patrician breed. She is in full possession of her faculties, as newspapers say of centenarians. Three rats learned this in the exodus at harvest. They will learn nothing else. 'What we haven't got, we'll do without' is good terrier philosophy, and the senior terrier demonstrates that if you cannot see them you can still catch them. Sometimes a turning ear and a growl indicate that she has heard a cat stamping its feet on the lawn; nobody else can.

She is teaching her successor to adopt a superior air towards the gundogs. This old-fashioned social barrier fits her generation. The gundogs are working class. Terriers are members of the household. Not only the fact but the spirit of this distinction must be maintained, and will be while there is breath in her body. Perhaps this will not be for very long. We have shared much together, times of ecstasy and desolation, but chiefly of bright contentment. She has cheered me by some of her triumphs and adventures, and I have wished I could have done something to inspire her in return. We have dug and hunted together. I have known the pleasures of her childen, and she has given her heart to mine. When we part she will leave me incomplete, but richer for her comradeship.

One can think too much of the future.

On Buying a Horse

The only near-certainty about the deal is that one gets either less or more than one pays for

ONE TRANSACTION DOES NOT ALTER. IT IS THE SALE OR, TO PUT it more bodefully, the purchase of a horse. Mankind's astutest brains have borne upon the matter across the centuries. There is one near-certainty about it. This is that the buyer of a horse does not acquire what he pays for. Go to market and put down £80 for a bullock, and all present will agree that one gets £80 worth of bullock to within 50p either way, no more, no less, at the prices ruling in the place and on the day, precisely that. It is different with a horse.

Go to auction or do a deal to buy a horse for £300, or £2,000, or £20,000, and all present will agree on one thing only; the buyer needs his head seeing to. Dark and numerous will be the cautionary tales, once the bargain has been struck, of past history and future hazard. Hence the frequent recourse after such decisions to that prince of nerve tonics, whisky. The rawboned four-year-old which slimmed your wallet by £300 is worth almost anything, except £300. It throws two splints in a month, has to be turned out for six, and is roaring when taken in again. It takes a chap like a QC on the next rostrum to squeeze £150 for him. Or perhaps it reveals a pop like a grasshopper and you spend the next decade wondering why you let it go show-jumping for a mere £1,000. The £2,000 six-year-old is not worth it either. Far from it. He wins three hunter-chases on the trot, almost literally, all by eight lengths or more and poses the agonising question of whether to take £12,500 to which an ace trainer will go, or wait for a better offer. Or perhaps he is duck-hearted, and becomes a patent-safety for £600.

As for the £20,000 yearling, we all know what happens to

him. In his first two-year-old stakes he runs green and makes no show. In his second he hates the mud, and makes no show. In his third he cannot act on a left-handed course, and makes no show. In his fourth he just makes no show, and nobody any longer cares why. At £800 and added to the list he fades away, to reappear in a new name as a show hack three years later, having been resold twice for less each time, or he wins a Classic and is syndicated at a quarter of a million.

These daunting thoughts invade my mind to recall the awesome possibilities which await those who buy horses. They loom the larger because, in a manner of speaking, I recently bought one. The purchase introduced measureless extra unknown quantities. It was a pony for the children. Beside a pony, even a horse is comparative simplicity. Whether a Classic candidate or a confidential cob ('suit nervous lady in seventies'), the requirements are at least equine. It is different with a pony.

As every father knows, a pony for the children must have human and mechanical qualities, too, including the benignity of an archdeacon, the paces of a ballerina, the prudence of a butler, the durability of a prop-forward and the adaptibility, though not the appearance, of a lunar module. Such a paragon is difficult to find, to put it mildly. When found, after months of search and repeated disappointment, *pater familias* is apt to be something near a nervous wreck, the victim of every insecurity from wild surmise to rank suspicion.

The charming family with whom it has done time suddenly seem less real and more apparent. What if their social ease and general pleasantness are cloaks assumed to hide more sinister characteristics? Are they, perhaps, a wily and grasping clan, of deep financial acumen as well as histrionic talent, passing on pony after pony to their handsome profit? When a horse looks over the door, charity flies the yard gate. Nevertheless, the moment comes when the two outwardly urbane heads of families assume the traditional attitudes of contestants in man's most testing duel of wits. The gimlet-look sharpens the eyes of the otherwise blandly assured vendor until even Genghis Khan would quail. The buyer flexes his muscles for that semi-turn of the shoulders in the direction of the car, timed to the split second, which interrupts the routine stuff about sending him back if you don't like him (just try it, with a family of daughters freezing the atmosphere, and well the seller knows it).

Finally, with a suddenness which is both relief and climax, the thing is done, all passion spent. What we gave for the pony is my affair. Now I am wondering what he is worth. Time will tell.

Night Mare

SIR,

My son owns a 16.1hh, almost pure thoroughbred mare, trained as a show-jumper and now training as an eventer. She is quiet and well-mannered, lively and keen. Often, at night, she will suddenly whinny loudly. If we go to her she appears contented but alert. She is not hungry. The only explanation we can think of is that she has been dreaming. Is this common in horses?

ELIZABETH BUCHANAN
Portman Square, London, W1

Good British Apple Pie

How to ensure its unending succession from August to June, all from the home orchard

ACCORDING TO A RECENT GALLUP POLL, APPLE PIE IS ONE OF THE two most popular dessert dishes, which puts to scorn all those jeremiahs who say that the nation is in decline. No nation can be in decline that eats apple pie. If we grow the right varieties on dwarfing rootstocks we can have a succession of cookers that will see us through from August to the following June, given good storage and garden space for half a dozen or so trees. With fewer trees there can still be enough apples to make a variety of dishes for at least three months, using apples that are rarely grown commercially, and thus are seldom seen in the shops.

Such a choice would exclude three of the best known, Early Victoria, Grenadier and Bramley Seedling, but there is no reason why these should not be included. Bramley, mighty grower that it is as a standard, can be reduced on M9 rootstock to a tree that a child can pick from. It will, if firmly staked, remain in production for many years and will produce around 60 good-sized apples, or about 25–30lb, in a favourable year. It must, however, be planted well away from any pockets of frost in the garden.

Leaving aside the popular commercial varieties, the season starts in August with the beautifully flowered Arthur Turner. This is becoming popular with fruit farmers, but it still has a long way to go, and is not yet abundant in the shops. It is in season from August to October, giving medium-sized apples from the early pick and large ones later. Cropping is regular, the apples are greenish-yellow with a brownish cheek, and the tree is nicely compact. Starting in late August or early September and remaining cookable until December is Stirling Castle, one of the best of its season. A hundred years ago, some forty after its introduction, a Herefordshire grower called it 'a gem of apples', an opinion not to be brushed aside, for Herefordshire men knew a thing or two about apples.

There are two cookers of outstanding quality for September to October, namely George Neal and Golden Noble.

They are practically never seen in the shops, and it is doubtful whether they would be used in mass-produced apple tarts, which at that season are more likely to contain unripe Bramleys, or Grenadier, which is then ready but is not in the same class, or long-spent Early Victorias. George Neal and Golden Noble combine beauty with quality. The first is pale yellow, often with an orange flush, and the second is somewhat lemon-coloured, cooking to a golden froth. These are two of a number of varieties which disprove the fairly widely held notions that cooking apples must be green, and that one

variety is much the same as another. To the discerning palate
there is as much variation as there is among dessert types,
and it is a fact that some of the best flavoured and textured
cooking apples are not green-skinned.

Warner's King, for example, in season from October to
January, is one of the finest for baking, and is a pale greenish-
yellow. Any garden-size tree should manage a regular annual
production of at least two dozen fruits of baking proportions.
Another yellow-skinned apple, and one which can reach a
pound in weight, is Peasgood's Nonsuch. This has an attractive crimson flush with darker stripes, soft, yellowish flesh,
and cooks to a melting froth. It is in season from September
to November.

For storage well into the New Year we have several apples
of the highest quality. I would hazard a guess that the least
known, yet one which is perhaps the only candidate as a rival
to Bramley Seedling, is Woolbrook Russet. The only green-
grocers' shops anywhere in Britain where it will be found (if
at all) will probably be those supplied by a local gardener.
Its background is half dessert and half culinary, the latter
part being Bramley, and the former King's Acre Pippin,
which is itself reputed to be a cross between Sturmer and
Ribston Pippins. It thus has rich blood in its veins. It does
not look a bit like a cooker, which is possibly one reason why
is has failed to make an appeal to the public, but as an apple
keeping until April it can hardly be bettered for flavour.

For frosty gardens Crawley Beauty and Edward VII are
first rate. The former blooms in early June, when all danger
of spring frosts is over, and the latter, though blooming
rather earlier, is usually late enough to escape. If the colour
of cooked apples can heighten gastronomic anticipation, then
few varieties should be capable of performing this function
better than Edward VII, which cooks to a rich red froth. It
is said to be a cross between Blenheim Orange and Golden
Noble, so should provide richness indeed. With good storage
it will keep until April. When I grew Monarch on Surrey
green-sand it kept in perfect condition from November until

May. It is a splendid apple, though inclined to biennial bearing. The wood is rather brittle, but careful formative pruning will build a strong framework, when any breakage that does occur will be confined mainly to the fruiting laterals, rather than to the much more important wood of the scaffold. An essential factor in building a tree of this variety is to select the main framework leaders only from shoots that grow out at a wide angle to the stem.

Latest of all there is Annie Elizabeth, which is still cookable in June. It is a large, pale yellow fruit with a red flush, and the deep rose-coloured flowers are extremely decorative. This apple has the unfortunate habit of shedding its load suddenly, just before picking time, though with a little experience one soon learns to beat this, if only by a wind's breath (although the crop will often fall, wind or not).

Readers whose apples go rotten after a few weeks in store will probably think my storage periods are optimistic. They are not, provided the crops are picked at the right time, and that only completely undamaged specimens are stored, and then somewhere that is frost-proof, free of smells, slightly damp, rather than dry, and with a temperature as near as possible to 37°F.

Rig of the Day

A heart-felt plea for frankness in the matter of what one is expected to wear

AT SUNDOWNER TIME MY WIFE WAS ENGAGED IN THE WOMANLY task of putting extra holes in stirrup leathers. Without envy I noted that it was too important to delegate to me. From her silence a man might have supposed that her thoughts were concentrated on what she was doing. But he would need to be a bachelor. 'Charmian's coming in trousers,' she said.

It was one of those *volte face* remarks, like the old-fashioned psychic bids at bridge, which wives employ to test the IQ of their spouses. Experience teaches one not to hurry, but to assess possible motivations and ramifications in a mature way. Taking a sip or two to gain time, I appreciated the situation. The reference was clearly to Sunday lunch. Evidently the information so succinctly conveyed was of significance, or it would not have obtruded on such a moment. And inferentially it concerned me. How?

If Charmian wore trousers, presumably I had *carte blanche* to wear trousers, too. But since this is my invariable practice, an announcement hardly seemed necessary. There was more in this than had met the ear so far. After a further sip or two, to allow the tension to build up, I said invitingly, 'And?'

'Well, in that case,' the words came from a face taut with concentration, 'you can't reckon on John wearing a suit.' I had not, until then, done any reckoning at all on this point, and it did not seem the moment to start. I put the ball back in the other court. 'How many more holes will you put in?' I asked. Answer came swift and positive.

'So you'd better not wear a suit either. Are any of your more decent jerseys clean by any chance?' Ignoring the aspersion, I accepted what was plainly an operational instruction.

In the event, not only was one of my decent jerseys beyond reproach, but so was one of John's.

The thought remains that indications of what is expected are too often vague, too easily dispensed with. Evening Dress with Decorations: Carriages at 10.30 does very well for formal occasions. At least there is clarity about Black Tie, Decorations, inappropriate as this uniform of the permissive society continues to seem. When one passes to the private sector, so to speak, the era of crumbling conventions raises doubts on every side.

While claiming no particular virtue, I prefer to be properly dressed. To do so is generally to be more comfortable, in every sense of the word. How many contemporaries would agree with me I have no idea, but I still regret the passing of the boiled shirt and dinner jacket, and regard the soft front and tuxedo as one pace taken to the rear. To don a stiff shirt was not really very difficult. It is still done by thousands without comment whenever they put on mess kit. And once one is inside, and the cold surfaces have warmed up, it enhances the sense of occasion. By contrast the tuxedo is a garb of unfulfilment, as though one had already dined without knowing it and had now put on pyjamas.

But it is essential that whatever is to be worn should be clearly indicated at some recognised stage. It is simply not good enough that it should merely leak out in crypticisms from a lady otherwise engaged, say in adding holes to stirrup leathers. Preoccupied or less receptive husbands might miss the message. The marvel is that I didn't. Moreover the boot can be on the other foot. How often, as the years pass, have I returned with the news that we are to dine with the So-and-so's and walked right on to the inevitable question, 'Well, for goodness sake find out if she's wearing a long dress'. The time is long overdue for an understanding on this matter.

At present the telephone system is strained by husbands communing among themselves. Some are ferreting out the required information. Others are checking it. All know that whatever they discover will be checked again, rechecked and cross-checked by their ladies before it is acted upon.

In admiration I salute a forthright friend in the down-to-earth county of Yorkshire. His invitations to stay are wont to include intimations of whom will be coming for dinner, ending bluntly, 'and I shall be wearing a dinner jacket'. This does more than crush uncertainty. It indicates that his house, thank heaven, is not one of those where dinner is compatible with turtle-neck sweater and jeans, as it regrettably is in some. And with true Yorkshire regard for other people's independence it concedes, by avoidance of direct stipulation, that his guests may wear what they like, but that they will look damn fools if they do not dress as he does.

A Tight Jury

When twelve gentlemen of the jury appeared in court last week, only ten, ranged five to a row, could fit in the appointed box. Two of ampler proportions sat on chairs in front and not unnaturally felt a loss of gravity there.

The problem raised certain questions. Are jurymen becoming broader on the beam? Is there a standard size for jury-boxes? Was this one regularly a ten-seater? Is there a move to decimalise the jury? Alarm was happily assuaged.

The box was not a proper jury-box but a makeshift in the Queen's Building of the Royal Courts of Justice. These were pressed into service to take the Old Bailey's overspill. But the Department of Environ- is appraising the whole layout of courts. Let it consider the matter in all its breadth.

The Soldier's Chorus

A song at twilight as the British Army knows it, and some speculation as to who first sang it

IT WAS HARDLY A SONG WITHOUT WORDS; BETTER INDEED HAD it been so. The subject-matter concerned the subsequent experience of one who had been sitting by Reilly's fire, eating chips and drinking porter. No good purpose would be served by quoting further. It will be familiar to all soldiery, past and present of all ranks, who have ever been within ear-shot of a sergeants' mess party. Whether it is equally familiar to the Royal Navy and the Royal Air Force is not known to me. We of the Army are inclined, in our modest way, to assume that the other armed Services are more refined or less robust or both. It is difficult to imagine such polite-sounding personages as engine room artificers and leading aircraftmen bawling forth in alcoholic fervour the lusty runes of a pongo.

The rune in question is mentioned here for the magnificence of the air to which it is sung. This combines tonal vigour with a musical inspiration comparable to its counterparts in *Faust* and *Trovatore*. Hearing the uplifting chorus afar off when arriving suitably late at an old comrades' supper, I confess to fearing what the neighbours might think. With relief I discovered that the organisers had shown the good sense to site the event at an erstwhile carters' inn a mile from the nearest habitation in any direction. This tactical remoteness ended all inhibitions on indulgence in martial melodies. The Great Wheel was rendered with timely *diminuendo*. This also is a ballad unlikely to be sung by bishops, and it is a piquant thought that some of their Lordships may remember it from campaigning days. With throats well flushed with ale we passed on to Mobile, Deolali Sahib, the

Little Harness Room across the Square, that dirge-like vale-diction now delicately watered down to Bless 'em all, and Thora Pani, Thora Char.

These were songs which resounded through countless campaigns. They are an elemental corporate voice of those who won all the battle honours of the British Army, of all the regiments of the living and the dead. Colours laid up in great cathedrals once flew among these rhythmic crudities to which fighting men give tongue, shocking though the thought may be to those who were never lonely, weary and imperilled far away with only basic memories to fire their muse.

The words, some of which would make a pornographer blench, have a modern or a timeless ring, according to viewpoint. If Shakespeare was right in his fictional reconstruction of camp-fire talk at Agincourt, soldiers' idioms have not changed much in 500 years. Perhaps soldiers' music is a lasting heritage too. That dedicated campaigner, Field-Marshal Lord Wavell, referred disparagingly in *Other Men's Flowers* to the folk songs of British troops. Here, for once, his appreciation seems open to question, especially if drinking songs are included. Any soldier whose knees are brown reckons to spend as much time drinking as marching and with pot in hand his spirit is set free.

If nobody is collecting the war songs of the British, somebody should start now. They are part of history. Their musical derivation is worth scholarship. Subtract those of evident camp-concert origin, generally based on hymn tunes or parodies, and there remain some which, unrecorded otherwise, must have been passed down by generation after generation of fighting men. The songs of crusaders and troubadours, not all saintly in their day, may be in the pedigree of those we sang in the lamp-lit, malt-fragrant Shades behind the carters inn while frost rimed the hedges under a starry sky. Ancient or modern, it was good to call again the tunes of the valorous if sometimes bawdy trade of soldiering.

Stillness on a Trout Stream

With the dry fly all things come to him who waits, given a little bit of luck

IN *A Summer On The Test* JOHN WELLER HILLS REMARKS: 'Cunning trout are caught by much watching and little fishing.' If this were true 50 years ago on such a river, how much more so is it the case today on those rivers where the stock is wild? Cunning trout are not necessarily the larger trout (larger, that is, than their local neighbours), but it is to be expected that many of them, having had sufficient time to develop the craft of self-preservation, are of good size. They lie in places where they are reasonably safe, where light or current or other natural conditions help to protect them. Maybe they move out at dusk to feed in the shallows, where they are more vulnerable, but most are relatively secure.

In 1924 the Test was not over-fished—certainly not on the stretches where Hills so much enjoyed himself—but the need to wait and watch existed, as it now exists everywhere except on streams where stew-bred trout provide 90 per cent of the sport. On remote rivers (for instance, in Canada) where rods are almost as rare as autumn daffodils, the need remains to watch.

Trout are curious creatures. Their behaviour throughout the world seems to follow the same pattern. No doubt they are more difficult to catch, day in and day out, on rivers where fishing is intense, but it is a fallacy to suppose that they are necessarily easy to come by on those that are scarcely touched. Wherever they live, trout are continuously threatened by one predator or another; after they have survived four years the few that achieve that age have indeed 'had their cards marked' and know how to look after themselves. There are more reasons than one why put-and-take fishing, even on a river, is dull work, not least the haphazard, crazy behaviour (resulting from lack of experience) of the unfortunates which are turned loose. Their conduct is in accordance with a nurtured childhood.

It is easy enough to recommend to a guest, on a river where the stock is moderate and fly is thin, that he should wait and watch, and even fill up time with a prayer; but when he believes that he is faithfully following the advice, he is still probably travelling much too fast. It is virtually impossible to go too slowly. On the most unpropitious day there will be a few fish on the move if one can but locate them. Often in such conditions the larger ones are more active than the smaller. It always seems curious that this should be so; perhaps, being more adventurous, they have waxed fat. They may show themselves only at longish intervals, and it is this that makes it important to mark them.

Fortunately, they tend to be 'bankers', which simplifies the matter of pinpointing them. The assumption must be that if a fish takes one natural fly in 10 or 15 minutes, it will take an artificial which floats properly into its parlour—a supposition which is usually correct. Some of us find it difficult to mark down a rise immediately and accurately, it sounds the easiest thing in the world, but it is not. It must be done the moment the rise is seen. It is useless to say 'Near that piece of green weed'. It must be precise.

To locate the trout is a welcome start, but far from the end of the watching game. What is he doing? Is he taking flies or hatching nymphs? Is he moving in search of them? Is he a slow operator or a brisk one? Is he selecting one particular kind of fly or taking any that come his way? Is he, perhaps, cruising? What will the current do with the artificial fly when it pitches in front of him? Come to that, which is his front? How soon will the fly start to drag?

Since the days of Hills, part of the watching procedure has been simplified. We are blessed with 'magic glasses', polaroids, which often, though not always, reduce the difficulties. With or without glasses there is a knack of seeing through water. Some people are much more adept than others at doing this. They are able, as it were, to ignore the surface, to penetrate the lower regions. By concentrating, by forcing their vision through the water and by taking time to study a limited area, they discover fish which others fail to see. Gradually, all kinds of under-surface movements and changes become apparent, until the river bed takes on a shape.

The belief that any visible fish is a potential riser has changed many a blank day into a success; every fish which can be seen without polaroids in the average river is catchable. A fish which is prepared to rise to a fly seldom lies motionless, as though asleep; he is constantly moving, maybe only slightly, doing little more than quiver, save when he makes sudden, sharp movements, as though something had attracted his attention, only to prove unpalatable.

The temptation to advance too quickly from one piece of water to the next likely place is difficult to resist. It arises especially on days when few trout are moving. But these are the very occasions when a more deliberate progress should be maintained, when every yard must be studied. The tiniest tell-tale ripple coming from the bank, the most fleeting 'unnatural' break in the flow, may be due to a vole or a gentle gust of wind, but it may point to a monstrous old trout enjoying a quiet meal.

But, of course, for every fish that is seen, tens, if not hundreds, remain concealed, and it is important not to disturb them, or, at least, to reduce disturbance to a minimum. There seem to be two distinct reactions by trout which are startled by movement on the banks. If the upset is not too sudden, or is of a sort with which they are familiar (as, for instance, when cattle go into a stream to drink), the fish will do little more than drift away to the far bank, then drop downstream for a few yards, there to wait until their lies are habitable again.

On the other hand, an abrupt or clumsy disruption of their peaceful existence has a different effect; it spells immediate danger, and whilst some will turn sharply on their tails to race downstream, many will scuttle away in the opposite direction, as fast as they can go, spreading a warning amongst their friends and neighbours upstream that something untoward is in the offing, and that they had better take evasive action.

Trout thus alerted leave their rising stations for the imagined safety of their sleeping quarters, in deep holes or amongst the bankside tree roots, and there are many rivers on which a lack of confidence thus induced will persist for two or three hours. It behoves the angler to dawdle quietly, even though he cannot achieve the harmless reputation of farm stock, not only because his immediate prospects will be improved, but also because the long-term result will be that, at the season's end, his fish will be much less habitually nervous and shy and therefore more catchable.

Malice on the Lawn

The great game of croquet provides fulfilment for the cads of both sexes

HUMAN NATURE INCLUDES GUILE, VINDICTIVENESS, PERFIDY, chicanery and spite. Since nothing is evolved without purpose, some may wonder what part these attributes fulfil in the general scheme of things. To me it is self-evident that they exist as fundamentals for the delicious and ruthless game of croquet. No form of contest is more misunderstood. In vulgar minds the traditional 'game of croquet at a vicarage garden party' is a synonym for endeavour of a milk-and-water kind. Those who believe this can have scant experience of vicarage garden parties, which are no environment for fainthearts, and none of playing croquet.

If the image survives of the prototype croquet player as being a maiden lady of gentility and seniority, none should under-estimate the arsenic-and-old-lace syndrome. In fact, of course, the great game is played by every sort and condition, including male persons of virile, aggressive aspect. Though it seems to be regarded as a rare eccentricity by those who broadcast or write in newspapers, my belief is that croquet has lately gained much in popularity. And so it should. As a means of exercising those resources of bile and spleen which we all possess, and which cannot otherwise be usefully deployed in civilised society, croquet transcends all other activities. In grace and poise it contrasts favourably with the contorted violence of golf, in mathematical combination it challenges chess, in accuracy and delicacy it compares with billiards, and in conversational possibilities it would make mincemeat of the Congress of Vienna.

My pleasure this summer has been to return to the lawn, and to discover that, in the past two decades, the less admirable traits of my character have not grown rusty by under-employment. Our family had a croquet tradition. One fore-bear played it almost non-stop from To Finish the Season until cub-hunting, declaring it to be the only reasonable summer pastime for a foxhunter too old for cricket. He played it, moreover, with disregard for ethics and mastery of the underhand which make croquet what it is.

The dissemination of alarm and despondency among the enemy, the nurturing of doubt and bewilderment, demand histrionic art and a sense of timing once the perquisite of high diplomacy. The tactical conferences between partners, when voices are lowered to invite eavesdropping, and then raised enough to release an inspired leak, could teach White-hall a thing or two. An impassive ox-like stare when an opponent is bent on mischief is the stuff of which trade union leaders are made. All human life is there.

What happens to the balls and mallets, hoops and pegs is no more than the thread which binds great ploys together. Croquet is a game of baleful plotting and hostile imagina-tion. The spoken word and the unuttered inference are its true currency. Nobody should play croquet who lacks a sense of humour. Nobody should be allowed to play croquet who is likely to abide by a sense of chivalry or magnanimity. Such would be too dull a fellow to engage the attention of those of more liberal views. Ladies who take part should be pos-sessed of barbed tongues, and a gift for distracting laughter.

Given these ingredients, plus a suitable side bet and a lawn which plays true while not devoid of interesting borrows, the scene is set for an English afternoon of idyllic rancour, especially if there are elms in the background and tea in the offing. Should the next world offer croquet I hope my wife and I can take on Al Capone and Lucretia Borgia. They would be in their element. Their side-talk might be interest-ing, and it would be a pleasure to dispatch them to those distant zones from which (except at upstage places like Roehampton and Cheltenham) the road back is long and hazardous.

Welcome in the Valleys

A Celtic author acclaims with fervour the pre-eminence of the Welsh inn

THE PUB IS AN ENGLISH INVENTION. THIS IS AN AWESOME admission for a Welshman to make, least of all about an institution evolved by recently arrived European immigrants, who still talk of England when they mean Britain. Nevertheless, it is true.

The Scot slakes his thirst in luxurious hotel lounges or bare bars. The Irishman behaves similarly and in country districts is often found in unlikely places like the back room behind a shoe shop. The Welsh, however, tend to follow the Anglo-Saxons. There is a big difference between a thatched inn in a soft Dorset village and one of harsher nature in the Cumberland dales. There are similar differences between Welsh pubs in the south and in the north. There is one common denominator, the beer.

For reasons inexplicable, the Scots made whisky, the Irish made whiskey and the Brythonic Celts made neither, so beer is perforce our national drink. In these days of tasteless brews from sterile metal containers, in the Principality one can still drink ale with the flavour of yesteryear.

Pubs in south Wales are places given to song and to long and heated discussion on coal, boxing and particularly Rugby football. There is always dispute about the past and generally hope and optimism for the future. 'Now listen. They've a young inside-half up in Abercynon, boyo, who is brilliant.' Acrobatic apparently, as well; 'Believe me, Dai, in a year or two he'll be ready to step into Gareth Edwards's boots as soon as he hangs them up.'

The only time there is a gloom on a Saturday night is if Wales has lost an international, and deep gloom only if it were against England. Name-dropping is a national pastime. There is not a south Wales man worth his salt who at around 10pm on a Friday night will not assert that the Chairman of Selectors is a personal friend who can give anyone two tickets for Twickenham in the morning. Name-dropping in Wales is easy. There are so few of them.

My close relative, Dylan, was of course the expert on Welsh pubs. During *The Outing* in the charabanc they visit 'The Mountain Sheep, The Blue Bull, The Dragon, The Star of Wales, The Twll in the Wall, The Sour Grapes, The Shepherd's Arms and The Bells of Aberdovey.' Dylan had a better ending than the one he used in that story. When the charabanc debouches its load at the Hermit's Nest, 'for a rum to keep out the cold', his uncle finds himself next to a stranger. 'I played Rugby for Wales in '08,' said the stranger. 'Liar,' said my uncle. 'I can show you Press cuttings.' 'Forged.' 'I can show you my cap.' 'Stolen.' 'I got witnesses to prove it,' said the stranger in a fury. 'Bribed.'

North Welsh pubs are more serious places, for north Wales is a different country. 'Where was that place, Aber-something, where there was all that fighting before the last war?' one man from the south asked another. 'Abergavenny?' 'No. No fighting there.' 'Aberdare?' 'No.' 'Aberystwyth?' 'No. No fighting there.' 'Oh Abyssinia.' 'Aye. That's right. Up in north Wales. Always fighting up there.

In north Welsh pubs they talk in Welsh and generally about sheep. They are awful poachers, as any man born south of Brecon will say, adducing the story of the American doctor, who, having been stationed in north Wales returned to do a little salmon fishing. After a week without even seeing a fish, he drove down to his old garrison town at the river mouth. The pub and the company there were unchanged and he was greeted like a long-lost brother. 'Been fishing, have you, Doc? Catching much?' 'I've not seen a fish these last seven days.' 'Oh, Doc, you should have let us know you were here. We'd have let one through.'

Monster in the Lane

The decline and fall of a great oak, and perhaps the birth of a place name and legend

AGAIN THE WOLF TREE REARS ITS UGLY HEAD. IT WAS ONCE A mighty oak. Lightning had blasted it long before it fell. Doubtless it stood upright for decades, drying and shrivelling in the wind, anchored with decreasing security by lifeless roots until some great storm laid it low. Down and out, it continues to resist obliteration. For longer than my lifetime it has lain on the broad verge at the edge of an unfenced wood. The stump of a snapped-off branch supports it, as if an old diehard were raising himself on an elbow for one last look at life. Each year it sinks a little further into the earth, and now the once great tree is almost prone.

The weather has worked so long upon it that it becomes less and less like a tree. The lashing rain of the turning seasons, sunshine in blazing noons, clinging ice and driven snow have given it the frailty of old age, and the pallor too. Whitened now, and jagged, it looks like some lean beast crouching to spring on passers-by.

Inevitably our daughters called it the wolf-tree, sublimating their fears by climbing over it in the Christmas holidays. Their friends have followed suit. When those friends, now children, have grown into grey village elders, and when the old oak has vanished, wolf-tree lane will be common local parlance among a generation now unborn. Then, no doubt, diligent men from far away will engrave Wolf Tree Lane on an Ordnance Map.

It will not be a new story. Fanciful views of the twisted limbs of fallen trees, gleaming palely through a winter twilight or looming like monstrosities against a setting sun, must have given identity to many a Dragon Green, Headless Lane,

Lion Hill, Ostrich Cross and Crocodile Corner. Deny it though we do, we are a poetic people. The bright imagery of children is immortalised for us in colourful names. To those in the know, reminders and check-lists are unnecessary. To analyse it, even with local knowledge, is an intellectual exercise. Sometimes it is speculative, sometimes original research. At the former level Bee Furlong, Owl's Castle,

Stew Pony and Frog Hall have exercised my mind. All have the freshness and incongruity beloved of youth. But this means little. A characteristic of the countryman is that he never grows up. Octogenarians keep their taste for schoolboy humour.

Even diligent inquiry has failed to unlock the secret of Bowerman's Nose on Dartmoor. Who is there with heart so dead that he can pass that primeval, upended rock without wondering who Bowerman was and what pecularity of size, shape, hue or texture earned his nose this immutable memorial? Somebody must know.

Tonight a north-westerly blows. Above torn clouds the stars are bright. Squalls alternate with moonlight which throws moving shadows from the tossing trees. Behind their headlamp beams the motorists know only the distinction between darkness and light. Those on their feet, as most men were when country lore was formed, see things differently. As place names grow, so do ghost stories.

As I came home across the fields a tall grey shape swayed soundlessly in front of me, suggestive of some priestly rite. A stranger, bursting thankfully into a local inn, might have told such a tale as would have established the presence of an unquiet spirit. I happened to know that trailing skirts of faded old man's beard hang from the top of a hedgerow at that point, even though I did not know until then what night can do to so everyday a sight.

Kendal Tears

Rain dripping—
Dribbling down the gutters—
Splashing on the pavements in the grimy grey town:
Tyres swishing—
Spraying scores of shoppers—
River's near to flooding, and a chocolate-brown.

Wet walkers—
Brollies at the ready—
Dodging up the ginnels as fast as they can go:
Child laughing—
Stamping in the puddles—
Loving every moment—but no-one wants to know.

IAN ENTWISTLE

Before the Morning After

Confronting a carefree occasion, a man may have a secret load on his mind

SOMETIMES IT IS NOT THE SPORTING EVENT ITSELF WHICH makes a memorable impression, but the events before and after. Being blessed or cursed with a strong sense of anticipation, my faculties are apt to approach their zenith as some long-awaited day approaches. They are at a peak the night before, when sleep, an essential before a day's grouse-driving or battue at high pheasants, does not come easily. An occasion arose when I was invited to fill another's place at an expensive pheasant shoot in the south of England and to stay in the house. I drove south from Yorkshire and arrived long after the other members of the party who had bathed, changed, dined and wined in gracious surroundings and with obvious satisfaction. I wished I had been there to share their enjoyment. As bedtime was heralded, the morning-calling slate was produced and plans were announced for the morrow.

I was put down for tea at 07.30 hours and I proceeded upstairs conscious that I was both wide awake and hungry. On the mantelpiece of my beshuttered room stood an imposing clock. As I undressed it slowly struck eleven times, accompanied by an asthmatic whirr. It proceeded to tick resolutely at a good marching pace until it reached the quarter, when it gave vent to another sonorous note. This was duly repeated when it hit the half-hour and began the long climb to midnight.

As the end of the day was sounding I leapt out of bed and examined the thing. It was old; old timepieces, I suspected, do not take kindly to being arrested in the middle of a run. I wrapped it in a large bath towel and put my head under the pillow. It was hopeless. The relentless ticking persisted and I waited agog for the next chime. In the end I carried the machine down the passage to a nearby lavatory and left it on the seat, trusting that no other inmate would chance upon it before I retrieved it in the morning. Sleep was slow to come, but some time in the small hours I dropped off, happy in the expectation that somebody would appear with that essential cup of tea at the appropriate hour.

I awoke to find a foreign manservant opening the shutters on a clear blue sky. 'Where's my tea?' I inquired. He looked blank and I glanced at my watch. Merciful heavens, it was ten to nine, and we were to leave the house at 9.15, ready for the day's shooting. The next 20 minutes passed in frantic activity until I subsided, bleeding from hasty razor slashes, over a plate of eggs in the dining room. My fellow guns regarded me sympathetically. One of them explained: 'You are down on the board to be called at 9.30, with breakfast in bed, which seemed odd, so we sent someone up to find out what you were doing.' I omitted to mention that the clock had disappeared, and it was not put back in my room the next night. I shot no worse than usual on either day.

A wartime leave nearly thirty years ago came conveniently over Christmas when the woodcock were in at home. They duly took the pride out of the young Desert Rat for a day or two, then plans were made to outwit the duck on the Shannon one dawn with some local cousins. Cartridges were scarce and my efforts had done damage to the stock. Petrol was non-existent, so three of us drove there in the pony and trap, resurrected for the duration. Twelve miles we went to meet the cousins who were to produce the cartridges at the meeting place. 'They load them themselves,' somebody explained, 'and there is apt to be a delay after you pull the trigger, so keep swinging the gun.'

This promised to make it doubly difficult for the moderate shot, but the thought of following a bird in anticipation of an explosion was interesting. I soon had my chance, the only one indeed, to practice the drill. A cock teal, oblivious of my presence behind a furze bush, came in to pitch in range.

I pulled the trigger and followed him down, dealing him a mortal blow as his feet touched the ground. 'Shoot them flying, lad,' shouted some senior relation, who, hearing no splash or thump, assumed that the officer had acquired unsporting habits in battle.

Irritated by this slur on an unblemished reputation, I dashed forward to pick my bird, only to fall headlong into four foot of icy water sinisterly placed in my path. I received no sympathy from the assembly, but they encouraged me to remove my nether garments and wrap myself in the horse rug which had been covering the pony. It was warm and fragrant to start with, but I was glad to get home.

East Riding Coast

Across the road, a hedge, a church,
A clump of birds'-nest-bearing trees,
Where rooks caw in the summertime
And gulls glide inland on the breeze
Which laps the waves that smack the rocks
Of Filey Brig and Bay.

But when the sea-fret rolls its way
Up Reighton Gap and Cayton Bay,
It hides the hedge, blots out the trees,
And makes the scene quite Japanese,
Veiling the face of Speeton's bluff—
The damp-white, seafoam-candy stuff.

And when the cold north-easter blows,
And claws at Bempton's mighty cliffs,
And winter seas crash Flamborough's heights,
And gulls scream round my house o' nights;
I draw my curtains, poke my coals,
And pray for all seafaring souls.

BERNARD CROFT

A Pride of Toppers

In which a radical view is taken of the male wedding guest's crowning glory

A WEDDING OVERHANGS US. TO MAINTAIN MORNING COAT, ETC, as summer grazing for moth larvae seems a stagnant investment, so here I am in some quiet rooms in Central London where men discreet as family solicitors supervise the sartorial glory of those detailed for marriages, Ascot, the Garden Parties and occasions of comparable formality; in other words, the dress-hire department of you-know-who. Thus far all has gone well. My reflection stares back at me from a long mirror. We confront each other eyeball to eyeball. The object is to assess the shape, fit and slope of a grey top-hat. A cousin looms up, preparing for the same great day.

'What are you putting that on for?' he asks ungrammatically. I tell him. 'Waste of money,' he responds. 'You won't wear it. No sooner put it on than you take it off again. Then you lose it. Never have one myself. If needed, soon find some other fellow's.'

Like that earlier and more famous wedding guest, his words leave me a sadder and a wiser man. Undoubtedly there is substance in his words. Yet they impose serious difficulties on those conscientiously resolved to do their duty by kith and kin. It would be unthinkable if base motives of cost and personal convenience precluded Our side from achieving parity in toppers with Theirs. Carried to extremes, total abstinence from toppers could leave our whole tribe bareheaded against the massed greys and lavenders of the opposition. I resolve that I shall do the right thing. I hire my topper as usual.

This emboldens me to put the point to my temporary technical adviser on wedding garments as we sign the lease.

His discretion does not wilt. 'Indeed yes, sir,' he responds, folding my temporary trousers with careless ease into a knife-edge crease, 'quite a number of gentlemen prefer not to take a hat nowadays. I think they find it a nuisance, sir.'

Reassurance that the hatless still rank as gentlemen does not tempt me to join their number. If a topper constitutes my responsibility you won't catch me laying it down. Won't you, though? Picture what happens.

In the sunlit lane outside the lych gate one unfolds from the car and dons the topper. Instantly femininity hems one in. Charm . . . gaiety . . . recognition . . . in less time than a sprinter needs to win an Olympic Gold, off comes the topper. It is long odds that it will ever go on again, at least until another wedding comes round. Its only useful function now is as a receptacle for gloves. Here my sympathies are with those who go on record as recognising the nuisance-potential of toppers. Placed under the pew seat it may or may not stay *in situ*. If it does it may well be trampled, dented or in other ways defaced. If it doesn't (and it won't unless the pew backs join the floor) it may be heeled like a Rugby ball two or three rows to the rear. The leanings, turnings, peerings and general restiveness of a wedding con-gregation mean that feet are never still. Out of sight is out of mind, especially with a topper.

Hence the ruthless common sense of my radical-minded cousin. If a topper is needed, as it will be, for a photograph or to wave amid the confetti showers as the happy couple drive away, there will be plenty around. Abandoned by the festive throng, pride of possession is short-lived.

Hence, too, that sad last duty of the ushers. As the shadows lengthen, and the first slammings of car doors begin their curfew on the day, these personable young men will make their final official appearance. Each with an armful of toppers they will go the rounds striving to reunite the jetsam of the occasion with the respective owners and tenants. Only the owners will be interested. And I bet there will not be many of them.

Queen of the Night

A walk by the light of the harvest moon, when past and present met

UNTIL STORMS END HER REIGN, THE HARVEST MOON CROSSES the sky in special glory. The sun is constant, and by common usage masculine. The moon's varied guises have given her feminine gender. She alters her image as the months pass.

For harvest she has a gentle brightness. Some of the reasons are obvious. In most years, the land is dry, humidity low, the atmosphere clear. Nothing dims the luminance of her second-hand sunshine; nor does anything add to it, as will later the reflections from frost and snow. Moreover, she shines upon a change of scene. Night dramatises what in daylight is mundane. Fields lately heavy and fences half-hidden with the ripened crops are now mown to stubble. Moonlight, whitening light tones and blackening dark ones, projects a countryside squared and ruled into a new geometry.

Hedgerow trees cast hard-etched shadows. For some of us these black patches still magnetise the eye. In such dark areas danger lay in wartime, now long ago. Beyond the shadows scattered bushes, windrows and bales which escaped the buckrake illustrate another quality of moonlight. In it objects change their shape if intently watched, and only seasoned campaigners can distinguish that which moves from what does not. To the inexperienced, a stick pile can become an armed man. The converse is also true.

High and clear in the empty sky, the harvest moon awoke alertness in me from which there is no escape. That capricious enchantress was infecting with half-imagined menace the innocent vales of southern England. Then, picking out the far-off skylines and tracks, my restless thoughts of war on this peaceful night seemed less than strange. King Alfred's

I

men had watched wind-twisted thorn bushes on the slopes below, and doubtless some of the newer recruits had seen them turn into armed men—sometimes in imagination, sometimes not. The skeletons of sixteen Danes, all beheaded, were dug up less than a mile away and not long ago.

A dark scar on the opposite breast of the valley was once the road which the Romans made from Old Sarum to Winchester. Along it the legionaries followed the eagle. Above it a great earthwork, still obstinately horizontal after 3,000 years, showed where an unknown people had walled themselves in during a time of trouble. Other eyes than mine had seen in moonlight what I could only imagine. They were far separated from me in time though not in place, and I felt fellow feeling for those long gone with unquiet minds. At that moment they seemed close, thanks to the moon.

Her beams may distort both vision and thought, but they leave some things clear. A wavering dot in the stubble below was a hare seeking for undersown clover. A barn owl, more than ever ghostly in the brightness, passed on noiseless wings. Not so two duck; they quacked and swished across the face of the moon. Dane and Saxon, Roman and Briton, watching through the anxious nights, must have seen their forebears pass. On these windy hills nothing much has changed.

It was time to go. A steep track down the lynchets led me safely home. Time had been well spent. Things seen by moonlight have a new perspective, and an extra truth. A chance to stand and stare in the gentle weather of harvest time had been worth creating.

Wanderlust

The ridge beyond the ridge I see,
That is the ridge that beckons me
On, on beyond the furthest hill
I speed like light, nor rest until
I see beneath me—blue and still
The calm and falsely smiling sea.

And yet this is a foolish lie.
In my own snug and sheltered sty
I hope to stay until I die.

But when on starlit nights I see
The Great Bear crouching over me
And some bright star upon the hill
The colour of a daffodil.
I fling my sober self away
And wish—before the break of day—
That I like Piping Tom could play,

'Over the Hills and Far Away'.

J. M. STEWART SCOTT

Owl at Day's End

In the fading light of autumn, a yelping told of a hunt across the furrows

IN A VILLAGE IN THE COTSWOLDS, A GLORIOUS AUTUMN DAY was almost over and the sun was dipping towards the darkening hills. A few scattered clouds, like lean, grey wolves, came creeping down the sky. In the fading light, the trees still glowed with blazing, bonfire hues, as if some inspired incendiary had set a torch to the October woods. Soon the oncoming darkness began to drown that lovely Gloucestershire landscape.

Faintly, across the fields, came the cries of owls calling to one another as they hunted over the newly ploughed earth. There was magic in that sound. Owls are such fascinating creatures, partly because of the wealth of folklore and legends associated with them down the centuries.

What superstitious beliefs relating to owls are regarded as tenable today, I wonder? The answer must depend upon who one is and where one lives. In the days of the ancient Greek Empire, an owl was the symbol of Athene, goddess of wisdom, and owls were generally regarded with favour. Not so under the Romans, who looked upon them with dread and detestation. Birds of ill-omen they were then. The imminent deaths of more than one Roman emperor were accurately predicted when an owl was seen to alight upon their residences.

Similar legends have come down right to our own times. It is not difficult to understand why most of them are sinister in character. Owls are active mainly at night. Some, like the pale barn owl, have a ghostly appearance in the twilight. Others, like the short-eared, have staring, lemon-yellow eyes. All are armed with needle-sharp talons. Among their favourite haunts are hollow trees, belfries, ancient ruins and other desolate places. Their flight is silent; they move like shadows among the shadows. Not all owl sounds are mellow or musical, like the tawny owl's hooting.

Only two nights before I had been disturbed during the small hours by the sudden shrieking of a barn owl just outside the bedroom window. The bird repeated its piercing cries for some minutes. It might have been called a rude awakening. It is not an attractive sound, but welcome to me, all the same. I have been interested in owls for many years. Barn owls in Britain, sad to say, have been declining in numbers. This one seemed to be in good voice. Good luck to it.

Cotswold country must be ideal territory for barn owls in their struggle for survival. Its vast, rolling fields provide an abundance of shrews, mice, voles and other small rodents upon which the owls pounce when quartering the ground in the autumn dusk. Farm outbuildings, nestling in the hollows, offer shelter and cosy ledges for breeding sites. At nearby Ablington there is a barn which is typical in this part of England. Ample as a church it is, with massive oak beams supporting the roof. Built of local stone it is an inspiring subject for an artist with a taste for ancient, country things. What more could a barn owl want? Only the friendly tolerance and understanding forethought of his professed friend and greatest foe, man. It is getting chilly. Black as a hat now. No moon.

Only a few lights gleam like the embers of dying fires from curtained cottage windows—and one in the telephone box. It is best to walk in the road if one cannot see. To think that a tawny owl, for instance—a little creature scarcely a pound in weight, with eyes almost the size of a man's—should be gifted with such marvellous night vision. Incredibly, barn owls can see to approach prey six feet away under illumination equivalent to no more than that given by a 'standard' candle at a distance of about 400yd.

Fires beside the River

*The robust world of the winter fishermen in the chill of a
Yorkshire dale*

WINTER HAD PERFORMED A SURGICAL OPERATION ON THE
world, draining colour from the sky and the hedgerows,
exposing the structure of trees. We opened the gate and drove
down a field towards the river. The grass was frosted, and
some sheep, huddling into their wool, browsed over it. We
noticed a car by the ford and three men setting up their
rods. Without admitting it, we felt mildly irritated that they
had got to the water before us. In this case, however, we
hoped for grayling, and our slight irritation stemmed from
a realisation that we could not, on that cold day, when movement was essential, rove the entire stretch of river. No
matter; the three anglers were going upstream; in the opposite direction were riffles and deep runs where there would
surely be fish eager for worms.

By lunch time we had not even had a bite. The sand-
wiches and coffee, normally a barely tolerable interruption to
our angling, attracted us. We returned to the car where
again the three anglers had anticipated us. They were
engaged in breaking down a hawthorn tree to feed a fire. By
their car stood a large yellow sack. 'Cop't owt?' said one. It
needed only that phrase to remind me: Leeds anglers. Years
before, I had regularly fished a river where a Leeds angling
association had the rights. Often, on Sundays, one or two
coaches would spill out fishermen by the village pub and I
remembered them as bluff, raucous, amusing, generous with
advice. 'Nothing,' we replied, 'perhaps it's too cold.'

'Why, yer want ter try ledgering wi' maggit; yer'll catch
nowt on worm.' One of them pushed a polythene bucket of
maggots towards us. 'Help yerself.' I had doubts; the fish

might tire of constant offerings of gentles. Worms seem, somehow, a more natural, even a fatter, more tempting bait. As for ledgering, I despised it as a dull, inactive form of fishing and believed roving could produce better results. 'Have you caught much?' I asked. 'About sixteen,' came the answer. 'Mostly grayling; one or two trout; all on maggit. Here, tek a few.' We did. After all, we could do no worse than we had done already.

The fire flared up. One of the men reached into the paper sack and drew out a handful of coal. Their preparation amazed us. 'Left our brazier here last time,' said another. 'Shoved it in a bush and it's gone.' The third angler, who had wandered down to the swaying suspension bridge, rejoined us by the blaze. 'Pike down thear,' he said. 'Quite a big 'un.'

We asked if they had ever caught one in this river. 'Aye, there were a 16-pounder we took out of an 'ole.' This was news; we had heard of the trout and grayling—even caught them—but no-one had ever talked of pike; certainly not so large. I cast into a fast stretch where the water streams from an eddy, curves over a line of stones and slips beneath the back-combing of the current. It is usually a place where one can visualise grayling ghosting the gravel and moving hungrily from side to side. But nothing disturbed my float. Behind me, pressing close to the far bank, a flotilla of mallard, five or six of them, paddled against the flow. A wren agitated a nearby bush. For the umpteenth time I reeled in. Two of the Leeds anglers wandered towards me. 'Mind if I cast in a yard or two above yer?' asked one. 'It's a good run this.' I had no objections and soon heard the plop of the ledger a few feet away. Then, almost immediately, there was a beating of wings as the mallard, all but one, took off. As if anchored to the bottom, the remaining duck circled, thrashing the water. From the hand of one of the fishermen dangled the pouch of a catapult. 'Good shot that,' he said. And as he went towards the bridge to retrieve it, I watched the mallard die.

I soon moved from that swim to a shallower run. Undoubtedly the fish were lying deep; the ledgering success proved that; but I wanted a change. Earlier I had thought of using a fly-spoon that a gipsy had sold me. There had recently been a report that someone had caught a number of large grayling on a spinner made from a pen nib. But I recalled that no spinning was allowed on this stretch of the Rye. Perhaps I should try maggot instead. Discarding doubt and worm, I put a few on the hook and cast in. Across the splintered light of the surface my float seemed to dip. One can never be sure: I struck, and there, finally, was the throb of a fish. But it was small; a game, out-of-season trout. Downstream, my friend had done better. To his borrowed bait a few grayling had fallen.

Meanwhile, I tried a relatively deep, turbulent flow. Between the green, pulsing weed beds something checked the float. I could feel the body of a grayling curving across the current and resisting the rod's pull. Slowly it came to the frozen net; not a large fish, but bright, active and cheering. Later, another fell to maggot and then, in the dusk, a third. My friend had a few more to his credit, all small, and none caught on worm. I passed the other fishermen, who now seemed intent on fishing the same piece of water. 'Caught anything?' 'One or two,' came the typical understatement. 'Nowt as big as last time. Me mate 'ere 'ad three on, one after t'other, from an 'ole down thear. Two pound each they were.' 'On ledgered maggot?' He nodded and smiled.

Shortly afterwards, when with cold fingers we dismantled our rods, we could hear the snap of branches upstream. They had started another fire. Overhead a rook flapped home and a small flock of mallard wheeled above the trees. Past the sorry hawthorn we could see three figures huddled by a warm glow. Almost shoulder to shoulder they fished on, resourceful, determined, and successful in their own way.

The White Light of Winter

Snow and the shooter, for whom a new dimension is added to the scene

CHRISTMAS APPROACHES, AND WITH IT THE PROSPECT, ALBEIT rather remote, of snow. Some abhor it, some, including children, yearn for it, and we sportsmen have mixed feelings. Those fortunates who live where they sport will usually welcome a reasonable fall; we who have to travel have memories of bad journeys to offset the beauty of a white countryside. For my part I will tolerate much inconvenience in return for the rewards; the marvellous quality of light created by the reflective white blanket; the sense of adventure as one walks through the strange, eerie landscape where familiar things now require consciously recognising; the strange quietness; footprints of wild things normally living unnoticed.

If I could order the weather, and fortunately I cannot, I would so arrange matters that on Christmas Eve I motored over dry roads to my holiday venue. On Christmas Day, given, of course, to the family, the snow would begin and by Boxing Day a cold sun would shine on a frozen, white world. We would go rough shooting, for this is the ideal sport for snow. Through the day we would pursue the pheasants, now grown strong and crafty, with the spaniels pushing out the hedgerows and the colours of the dead cocks contrasting vividly with the snow. At dusk, warm and content, we would flight duck by the river, growing colder as light left the sky.

Most of my teenage winters were spent in the High Peak of Derbyshire, which must be the best place for snow south of the Border. It was common to have snow cover lasting for several weeks and I still delight at the consternation of my Surrey neighbours when a fall lies for 24 hours. Each grey Sunday dawn would see me pedalling into the hills with a box of ferrets and an old hammer 12-bore tied to the cross-bar. In that forbidding world of rock and bare moorland grasses the rabbits rarely burrowed in soil but lived in the rock debris. When the ferrets laid up they could not be dug out and many a bleak hour passed waiting in the shelter of a dry-stone wall while the snow drove overhead.

In those carefree years I recall fishing the Dove for gray-ling as the snow fell so heavily that the maggots and hook would not sink but lay on the surface slush. The most vivid fishing memory is a day spent pike fishing in non-stop snow when the surface of the lake gradually froze until we were casting our live-baits into a hole of open water not 15 yards wide. That day the pike took with enthusiasm and ferocity, and as we killed them and laid them on the bank the pure white snow was stained a vivid red.

The two bad winters of our time have been 1946–7 and 1962–3. In the first I was denied any chance of sport, spend-ing it in the Artillery camp at Oswestry rehearsing the art of bringing 3·7in AA guns into, and out of, action. All the nearby RAF and Naval camps were closed and the inmates sent home, while we started each day by using our rifle butts to break loose our boots which had frozen to the barrack room floor overnight. During the interminably long, cold days I dreamed of chasing Norfolk pheasants and Derbyshire rabbits and tried to avoid losing a few fingers in the breech of the gun.

The second hard winter saw a different situation, for my shooting included a freshwater marsh on the Isle of Sheppey, and at the beginning of the hard spell I had marvellous sport by putting my head through a hole in a white sheet and let-ting it drape around me as camouflage. The journey on the first day of snow was difficult enough but I stepped from the car into the cruellest wind I have ever known—straight from the east and so cold I felt I could not endure it for long. The fact that, on several days, I lasted for more than eight hours is a tribute to the adaptibility of the human body. The cold was so intense that I built hides from ice floes on the Medway saltings, and the hares had dug small caves in the drifts on the lee of the dykes.

It was impossible to remain still exposed to the full force of the wind and sometimes I imitated the hares and scooped a cavity along the bank of a drainage ditch. The duck could not wait for dusk to feed but moved continuously during daylight to the summits of the little hills where the wind had

exposed frozen grasses. At dusk nothing moved and I waited by the regular flight lines in a frighteningly lonely world where nothing lived but the wind. After a few days it became obvious that we were in an exceptional spell and the priority moved from sport to the survival of the duck. WAGBI appealed to all wildfowlers to cease shooting and most did; some illustrating the love most sportsmen have for their quarry by going to much trouble and expense to put down food. A few argued that in mild weather there was little chance of a bag and when, at last, the weather favoured the fowler he was told to stop shooting. Personally when I shot the first duck showing signs of starvation I lost any desire to continue.

For this reason there is much to be said for the sudden cold snaps which favour the hunter but leave the quarry in good condition. I recall such a day on the Ouse Washes above Cambridge with a thick layer of snow, more falling, and the Washes frozen over except for a water-hole by which I stood. During the afternoon snipe appeared as miniature dive-bombers, black dots among snowflakes. When I hit them they just continued falling with closed wings and their own impetus broke through the thin layer of ice and snow on the foot or so of flood water. The retrieve was made by rolling up a sleeve, thrusting the hand through the hole in the ice and feeling hopefully. At dusk the widgeon came and the teal.

On balance I would rather shoot than fish in snow, for shooting is less static and the cold is more easily kept at bay. Even so, my best memories of sport in the snow belong to angling. When, in my late teens, I progressed from a bicycle to an elderly motor-bike I made several trips each winter after the pike of the Shropshire meres. Being almost penniless, I stayed in the hayloft of a small farm owned by a delightful old farmer with the perfect name of John Brown. Rolling into a single blanket, I would burrow into the hay, sharing the loft with various hens and strange things that went bump in the night. At dawn, near shaking with anticipation that today would bring the big one, I would search the loft for eggs, gather wood and fry them. Sometimes there would be snow and I picture now the smoke curling upwards, the eggs crackling in the pan and the white Shropshire countryside. Later I would drift in a small boat along the edges of the big reed beds, their stark brown spears softened with a coat of snow on the windward side, and spin with a home-made brass spoon with a bright red band painted across one side. Hang the inconvenience—let it snow.

A Stranger Here

Out of his depth and always a move behind the game, a husband faces an endurance test

AMID THE MANY CRISES OF WINTER, ONE AFFECTS ME personally though not solely. The passing weeks are fraught with menace. There is the serious possibility that I may be unable to avoid going shopping. In vain to plead, as is indeed the case, that I have already shopped in the present Anno Domini, and that immemorial custom has established me as a once-a-year shopper.

Women, however, are not readily persuaded. Even my wife, no hair-splitter on other issues, takes refuge in technicality over this one. On the occasion mentioned I bought two shirts, a transaction which had not been placed on the agenda. It is held that by thus exercising a beneficial interest I negated my immunity, and hence owe a full day's service at this vexatious and exhausting activity. The prospect is enough to make a man turn pale. It would have no such effect on a woman. Women, of course, go shopping almost every day. This means that they are in constant training, and fit to soak up punishment as they pursue the objects of their desire through endeavour, failure, danger.

Much talk nowadays concerns equality of opportunity for women. At shopping, so far as I am concerned, they can have it all. They will take it anyway. Women, even the sweetest and gentlest of them, can be awesome beings at a counter and to keep pace with them between one counter and another demands the eye for openings of a first-class jockey, the physique of a Rugby forward and the forebearance of a saint. It is these demands on physical and mental endurance which create the barrier between men and shopping, not the spectacle, to which we are all inured, of money slipping away.

My personal policy, often stated, is that the distaff side are welcome to take our entire expendable surplus and blue it *en masse* so long as I am not asked to accompany them.

However, in these pre-Christmas days fate entraps the most elusive of us. There again will be gloomy streets, probably gleaming wetly in the shortened afternoon of a London winter. Roaring traffic and gaudy light will weave their hypnotic spell. Within resplendent stores will be soft carpets, sibilant conversations, and the heady perfumes of purposeful femininity employing every aid to maintain morale.

'Gloves next, half right,' comes the hissed injunction and my wife is into her stride like a gazelle. Over such a line of country a woman, even if married to one, is as difficult to keep in view as a Leicestershire fox, especially when the glove department proves to have been resited half left. In the outer world life is no easier. 'Now for Hamley's,' comes the order. This will not preclude the helm being slammed to starboard and a sharp tack into Liberty's. It does not surprise me. Nothing does.

Not even the inevitable blockade on leaving a shop. The sequence seems frozen into an unalterable pattern. As we approach the portals which lead to freedom two ladies do likewise. I hold the door for them. They pass through. Insulated in the small world of their own thoughts, they are unaware of me. They halt, open their handbags, turn towards each other and consult. There they block the exit, keeping me marooned while my spouse foots it lightly towards the next battle of wits. Journeying home I shall speculate, as I have done for years, on the strange repetitiveness of this small scene. How comes it that time after time there are always two ladies in position for whom the door must be held open? Why do they time and again exchange views at the exact juncture which will immobilise everybody else. Must they be for ever oblivious to all except themselves?

As to the latter, why not join them? There can be only one salve for the rigours of shopping. Oblivion, in the home-ward train.

Heavens Above

Ten quiet minutes on a frosty night renewing some friendships with the stars

MY EYE WAS CAUGHT BY BETELGEUSE ON A COLD CLOUDLESS evening. In icy splendour, stars glowed and glittered from horizon to horizon. Having that rare boon, ten minutes to spare, I stood on the lawn and repaired some friendships. Orion was loping low to the south-east. Never here does he bestride the high sky as he does in the tropics. To see him thence, and to know that those at home could see him too, was a good thought in hard times to some of us who had acquired this impractical information.

In dry clear air far to the east of Suez, individual stars have distinctions lacking in our damp island. But, even here, Betelgeuse, red on the Hunter's shoulder, proclaims himself different from the rest. Indeed he is. With a diameter of 290 million miles he is big enough, were he hollow, for our earth to circle the sun in its present orbit inside him. Such magnitude and such distance are beyond the benumbed conceiving of such as me. The immensity of creation became an overwhelming thought, interrupted by a crick in the neck.

Impromptu star-gazing is not for those with much-bashed spines. If indulged in, the muscles must be eased occasionally. I eased mine by lowering the angle of sight. This brought me face to face with Sirius. He has a useful distinction. In emergency he may be recognisable independently of his constellation. A fair view of him through a gap in cloud can be enough to identify him even if no other is visible, to the solace of wayfarers and seafarers here below. A diamond brilliance in pulsating colours representing 25 times the luminosity of the Sun, establishes him. But this glory is kept for the desert air. Always low in our latitude, his radiance is seldom undimmed by the less clear atmosphere. But now, in still air and frost, Sirius put on a display worthy of a Himalayan winter night. He flashed white and green as if coding a message. The rays that carried it had left him just before the 1966 General Election. It was a pleasing reminder of better times.

The magnificence of half the universe made me ask myself why I stand and stare at it so seldom. Wiser men than I have looked at it long and lovingly since the birth of the human race with every motive from inevitable awe to analytical intelligence. In simpler times than ours, with fewer alternative preoccupations, the world's great backcloth challenged Man's thirst for knowledge. Hence the Arab mathematicians, far ahead of their time in the Roman era. But knowledge was not all, and must never be. Hence the fascination to less factual men, and mankind's debt for the riches of the arts.

By walking round the end of the house I might possibly have a view of Lyra. The constellation includes Vega, the midsummer star which inspired Richard Jefferies. Less than a week from Christmas, Vega was hard to find. Of course, I should have known. Lyra lies low to the North in winter. Demoted from the zenith where he is expected, Vega looked insignificant. Not so those faithful stands-by, the Plough, Cassiopeia and the Pole Star. They dominated the night in bold familiarity. The Pleiades were outshone. They come to view less readily in best visibility, when rivals otherwise unnoticed are seen round this beguiling little group which reminded Job of his place in the scheme of things.

For I was doing what men have done in all ages, replenishing my stocks of those components in life-style which run short from time to time. Wonder, humility and reverence all grow in the presence of the stars and in the realisation of some simpler truths about them. To imagine the universe is impossible without looking at them in silence and solitude. This limitless reality passes understanding. One cannot yet explain it by science, only by guess and by God. With the evidence before me, I prefer God.